Conversations in Time

Conversations
in Time

with men and women of the Bible

Herbert O'Driscoll

COWLEY PUBLICATIONS
Cambridge ⮀ Boston
Massachusetts

Published in the United States of America by Cowley
Publications, a division of the Society of St. John the Evangelist.
No portion of this book may be reproduced, stored in or introduced into a retrieval system, or transmitted, in any form or by
any means including photocopying without the prior written
permission of Cowley Publications, except in the case of brief
quotations embodied in critical articles and reviews.

Library of Congress Cataloging-in-Publication Data:
O'Driscoll, Herbert.
    Conversations in time with men and women of the Bible /
by Herbert O'Driscoll
        p.   cm.
    Includes bibliographic references.
    ISBN: 1-56101-155-X (alk. paper)
    1. Bible—Biography—Miscellanea. 2. Imaginary conversa-
tions. 3. Christian Life—Anglican authors.
    BS571.027   1999
    220.9'2—dc21   99-26295
                                                      CIP

Scripture quotations are taken from *The New Revised Standard
Version* of the Bible, © 1989, by the Division of Christian
Education of the National Council of the Churches of Christ in
the United States of America. Used by permission.

Cynthia Shattuck, editor; Annie G. Kammerer, copyeditor;
Vicki Black, designer
Cover art: *All Saints' Day* (1911) by Vasily Kandinsky

This book is printed on recycled, acid-free paper and was produced in the United States of America.

Cowley Publications
28 Temple Place   •   Boston, Massachusetts 02111
800-225-1534   •   www.cowley.org

For Paula,
with whom the conversation in time
has always been shared.

I also wish to say a particular thank you. These pages are my first attempt at sustained dialogue. As my editor, Cynthia Shattuck took that first attempt and, over many hours and days—yea, months—guided me in shaping something of much better quality and readability. I am deeply grateful for her time, her patience, and her constant encouragement.

Table of Contents

Prologue

Novelist L. P. Hartley begins his book *The Go-Between* by saying, "The past is another country. They do things differently there."

And in some ways he is right. When I was a boy at school in the south of Ireland, every Protestant child in the country had to take a religious examination. The examination came in three parts: one in Old Testament, one in New Testament, and one in church doctrine. The first two were common to us all, while the third would vary according to whether you were an Anglican, Methodist, Presbyterian, or Baptist. Such was its importance that in our school all other subjects ceased to be taught for at least two weeks before the examination day. From nine in the morning to three in the afternoon we would do Old Testament, New Testament, and church doctrine.

Such a regimen made it difficult for even the most unwilling student to avoid developing a fairly extensive acquaintance with the world of the Bible. For those of us who enjoyed this kind of study, the gift was magnified many times. Patriarchs and prophets, kings and queens, warriors and judges: all became our vivid companions. Many passages had to be learned by heart. It is simply not possible to recite aloud David's lament for Saul and Jonathan without in some sense encountering both the singer and the slaughtered.

And so for all my life afterward, through university and seminary, and in parish after parish, these men and women have journeyed with me, their past always my present, their faces vividly imagined, their voices clearly heard, their presence closely felt.

The past is indeed a foreign country, but what I have come to learn is that in some ways it is a familiar country, too. In recent years I have had many imagined encounters with figures of scripture, some of them individuals who fascinated me in my youth and others who only came to me in middle age. Meeting them, seeing them in the mind's eye and listening to their voices, was effortless because they were always in some sense present with me and in me. But the challenge was to share these encounters with you.

As I thought about where I might meet each of these men and women of the Bible, I decided to place the encounters in the kind of setting and circumstances where they might be found if they lived as my contemporaries. For instance, when I write of Deborah, judge in northern Israel in the twelfth century B. C. E., I place us both in an auditorium where I have just listened to her lecture on women in modern Israeli public life, whereas I find Nehemiah beside the walls around Jerusalem he himself had rebuilt. As soon as this decision is made, I begin the conversation, or, for that matter, they begin it!

And that is how I have come to see that even though the past is another country, some elements in the landscape are not so different from our own.

Thus this book was formed, chapter by chapter, encounter by encounter. As to why one person was included and another not, I can only answer that I introduce to you the friends who happened to be in my company as the book unfolded. I have many other friends but I cannot speak of them all, nor is it possible to assemble them all in one place for introduction. Again, I may disappoint those who wish to take away some teaching from each of these encounters. The men and women of the Bible have for so long carried the weight of our teaching and moralizing that it prevents us from meeting them as people, unencumbered. I wish with all my heart to free them from these burdens. I wish to allow them to be themselves, immensely interesting and vibrant human beings, living the most human of lives.

My hope is a simple one: that I, who was given the gift of the company of these wonderful people from childhood, might offer them to you as the best of good company for your further journeying.

◦

1

Abraham

The Patriarch

Now the LORD said to Abram, "Go from your country and your kindred and your father's house to
the land that I will show you. I will make of you a
great nation, and I will bless you, and make your
name great, so that you will be a blessing. I will
bless those who bless you, and the one who curses
you I will curse; and in you all the families of the
earth shall be blessed."

(Genesis 12:1-3)

Crossing at Taba from Israel into the Sinai is always a
risk. You have to remind yourself a number of times
that these two countries, Israel and Egypt, have signed a
peace agreement. When you eventually move past the
checkpoint and the careful questioning of the Israelis,
you walk across the actual border, loaded down with your

lighter pieces of luggage, to the narrow entrance of the Egyptian army huts. This time you hand your papers a number of times to a line of bored and humorless faces. Almost no words are exchanged. You emerge from the sweltering huts feeling extremely tense, as I did, and longing to be on your way.

At this moment all I yearned for was a smiling face and a welcoming voice. Suddenly there it was. In front of us the Land Rovers were parked, and our guide had stayed in the shade of the first vehicle until my tour group emerged from the checkpoint. He got down and came forward, arm outstretched. A few words of friendly greeting, a few remarks about the bureaucratic hassle we had just been through, a signal to the drivers to load us into the Land Rovers, and we were off, swept along between the dark rock faces of the area on our right and glimpses of the blue water of the Gulf of Eilat—or of Aqaba, depending on whether your viewpoint is Israeli or Jordanian—on our left.

On the evening of the second day we were deep in the Sinai, and by then we knew that we were in experienced hands. Our guide stood out because he was the oldest (our drivers were all in their twenties). Each evening he took charge of preparing the evening meal. With the most basic utensils, a limited variety of ingredients, and an oven that was little more than a depression in the sand, he produced mouth-watering dishes of lamb, eggplant, yogurt, and rice. But I noticed something more than this. It was obvious that the young men of the desert who delighted in hurling across the rough terrain in Land Rovers, with cigarettes dangling and head dresses flying in the hot wind, looked to him with a certain deference, a sense of respect.

I am not quite sure when I first figured out who he was. I succeeded in making an opportunity to chat the night before we would begin the journey out of the desert towards the coast. He smiled across the fire when I said, "You must know the desert like the back of your hand."

"When you've traveled as much as I have, you can't help knowing it!" our guide replied.

I sensed an invitation to go a little further. "Has it been a long time since you were last here?" I said, feeling my way carefully.

"Yes," he said, "it has indeed been a long time. It's good to be here again." For a moment he hesitated, then asked, "When did you realize who I was?"

"Yesterday. I wasn't sure, but I noticed the way the others treat you. Almost as if they knew."

"Perhaps it's because I dealt with many like them. They herded sheep for me, tended my camels, fought skirmishes. My sister's son Lot was their age when we first came into these parts. In those days you didn't dare pass through here alone, so we traveled as a tribe, a small army."

"You passed through here with Sarah, didn't you?"

Abraham looked out into the starlight beyond the low fire. "Believe it or not, we came right through here, this very same *wadi*." He seemed to be about to say more but he stopped. The silence was so long I wondered if he hoped I would leave, but then he very quietly spoke into the darkness.

"When we first came through here," Abraham paused, looked out towards the end of the *wadi*, and smiled, "we had plans and great hopes." Only then did he turn towards me.

"Why did you come down here at all?" I had always been curious about this part of Abraham and Sarah's story, and now I had a chance to find out.

"Simple," he said. "None of us could ignore the Egyptians, especially if we wanted to assemble large land holdings anywhere near this part of the world, and that is what I was trying to do in those days. The Egyptians were always wary about their northern borders anyway; I decided it would be good politics *and* good business to make myself known. The other reason was that we might well need their corn someday. You never knew when famine would hit in southern Israel."

"And of course it did." I was thinking of the time that Abraham and Sarah went down to Egypt during one such period of famine and lived there as resident aliens. As the book of Genesis told it,

> When he was about to enter Egypt, he said to his wife Sarai, "I know well that you are a woman beautiful in appearance; and when the Egyptians see you, they will say, 'This is his wife'; then they will kill me, but they will let you live. Say you are my sister, so that it may go well with me because of you, and that my life may be spared on your account." (Genesis 12:11-13)

"You're wondering—," he hesitated, searching for words, "you're wondering about the story we had to make up about Sarah and me."

"Yes," I said. "It couldn't have been easy." It was my turn to tread carefully. I could feel his wariness.

"Obviously neither of us liked the idea. Who would? But the fact was, we were heading into a situation where we would be totally vulnerable if the Egyptians decided

to make trouble. I knew that as a major foreign landowner I would be looked over by the Pharaoh at least once.
That meant he would see Sarah, and I knew what could
happen to me if he decided he wanted her."

"You mean you could have been murdered?"

"Of course. My death would have been a mere administrative detail for the Egyptians. Neither of us wanted
that."

"So you passed her off as your sister."

"Yes," he said, "I did." That was all he would say. He
resolutely kept his gaze straight ahead.

But I couldn't keep my curiosity in check. "Did you
have other wives?"

"Of course," he said patiently, as if addressing a child.
"Of course I did. That was the custom. The times
demanded that there be many children. Our children
and their descendants strengthened the tribe both social-
ly and economically, gave it additional prestige. But what
I felt for Sarah was always different."

I noticed how often he spoke her name. "It must have
been tough on you both when no child appeared, especially a son. It's obvious from the Bible that you thought
about it a great deal. Did Sarah?"

"Very much," he said. "But after a certain point we
didn't talk about it anymore."

"So you had a child with Hagar instead."

For a moment he was silent, almost as if he were not
going to answer. But when he spoke he seemed quite at
ease. "Hagar was a fine woman. I liked her. I didn't love
her, but I thought enough of her to feel sad for her when
Isaac was born, and she and the child had to go."

"In the records there is a suggestion that someone
looked after Hagar in the desert when she left the camp.

The Bible speaks of an angel calling to her in the wilderness and leading her to a spring of water, and of God looking after Hagar and Ishmael in the wilderness as the boy grew up. Was that your doing?" I asked.

"I'm glad you caught that," he said. "I'm glad because it's true. I arranged that she would be all right until the child was grown and strong. It was the least I could do. I think Sarah suspected sometimes, but she never said a word."

"What do you think eventually made Sarah's pregnancy possible?"

"I honestly think it was the fact that we had both given up hope. At least, we had both decided that it was not in the Lord's plan. We had accepted things as they were without necessarily understanding *why*, and then, in the way that life sometimes plays out, it just happened. Perhaps it was important that we never thought of ourselves as other than in God's hands." He looked upward as he said this, then looked at me as if gauging the capacity of a western visitor to understand such blind trust.

I decided to risk deep waters again. "And the time you nearly lost him? Isaac, I mean. The time you felt it was necessary to—" I found myself searching for a softening word— "to offer him up. Can you talk about that?"

"I can talk about it," Abraham said, "mainly because I didn't have to go through with it."

"You mean because of the ram caught in the thicket?"

"Yes, but something had been there before the ram. Something inside myself yet also beyond and above me. I think in that moment God revealed something about himself to me. I realized with blinding clarity that the Lord did not want my child's life. He wanted *my* life, wanted it in total obedience and faithfulness. The ram didn't so much change things as it became a means of *my* changing things."

His gesture towards the sky made me realize that the stars were dimming very slightly. Somehow I knew that this kind of conversation would not be offered again. "You and I need to get some sleep," I said, "but just one thing before I let you go." I swept my arm in the general direction of the northern and eastern horizon. "Knowing what you now know about this part of the world, about all that has happened here—the hatreds, the wars, the killing—is there anything you would have done differently?"

"I would have brought Ishmael home from the desert." His answer came without the slightest hesitation. "I think if I had made up my mind to do it, Sarah would have agreed. It would have been hard to persuade her, but I think she would have gone along. Think what a difference it would have made in this part of the world if Isaac and Ishmael had grown up as brothers."

I reflected on what Abraham said. We sat in silence, each of us thinking about a long history that could have turned out so differently: the armies that never would have marched, the countless people who would not have died, the hatreds that might never have been born. Eventually he heaved himself up to a standing position, dusting the sand from his once white, long apron.

"Sleep well," he said as he moved away from the last embers of the fire.

"And you," I replied.

I stayed awhile, knowing that sleep would not come easily. When I eventually moved towards my chosen patch of sand, Abraham had slipped into his sleeping bag and become one among the small dark mounds around the parked Land Rovers. In the days that followed, we encountered one another at the journey's mealtimes, but by some unspoken agreement we never returned to our conversation.

2

Jacob

The Operator

When Esau heard his father's words he cried out with an exceedingly great and bitter cry, and said to his father, "Bless me, me also, father!" But he said, "Your brother came deceitfully, and he has taken away your blessing." Esau said, "Is he not rightly named Jacob? For he has supplanted me these two times. He took away my birthright; and look, now he has taken away my blessing." Then he said, "Have you not reserved a blessing for me?"

Isaac answered Esau, "I have already made him your lord, and I have given him all his brothers as servants, and with grain and wine I have sustained him. What then can I do for you, my son?" Esau said to his father, "Have you only one bless-

ing, father? Bless me, me also, father!" And Esau
lifted up his voice and wept.

(Genesis 27:34-38)

I n recent years I have increasingly found that I am
invited by old friends to officiate at the weddings of
their now grown children. Invariably I say yes if I possibly can, and that is how, a few months ago, I found myself
at a very happy occasion. A young woman whom I
remembered as a child in a previous parish of mine was
getting married.

Among the guests were a number of young profes-
sionals: lawyers, bankers, realtors, marketing and adver-
tising people—that kind of gathering. During the toasts
I became aware of one of these young men standing
quite near me as we all listened to a long succession of
speeches. During one of the breaks, to my great surprise,
he approached me, wearing a well-cut suit, smiling, and
carrying two glasses of champagne. In his late twenties,
he was thin and very fit, with a tan that at this time of
year means regular skiing.

"I noticed you didn't have a glass for the toasts!" He
was friendly, very much at ease with people. After he
handed me the glass, the young man remained beside
me as if to chat. This should have alerted me to something, because youth does not often single out age for
conversation unless there is a particular reason.

He was looking over at the couple when he said soft-
ly, "They've known each other for about a year. I wonder
how they would respond to the idea of waiting around for
each other for seven years?"

I knew immediately who he was. "Jacob!" I said. "Am I right?"

"You got it," he laughed. "I guess it was the seven years that tipped you off."

"Yes," I said, "I've always thought seven years was a long time to hang around for a bride."

He shook his head. "Not for Rachel. She was worth every minute of it. Why don't we get out of here and find a quiet corner. I'd love to talk."

"I've always thought of you as someone who—" then I checked myself because I realized this conversation was going to be a little tricky. After all, I was face to face with someone whom I had never liked: Jacob had always sounded very unpleasant in the Bible and yet now he was being extremely pleasant to me.

He certainly made it easy for me, and I could see why he was successful with people. There was an ease and a charm about him that was hard to resist. "You know my story," he said. "Believe me, I have no illusions about myself as I was back then, any more than you do."

I smiled. "One of the things I've learned in life is not to make quick judgments. Tell me about you and Esau."

He shifted a little in the chair. "It's simple, in a way. I cheated him out of his inheritance from our father, and then I spent the rest of my life regretting it."

"You mean when you were still boys at home and you got him to sell his birthright?"

"Not to mention robbing him of Dad's blessing." He was silent for a moment, and then perked up. "But, you know, I've never liked being stereotyped as a crook for all time just because of a few things in my misspent youth!" He grinned at me.

I knew I was taking a risk. "I hate to say this, but your misspent youth was not the only time you used people for your own ends," I said. "I know I'm being blunt, but I also know this chance to talk won't last very long."

He took it well. "You mean the years with my Uncle Laban? Remember I took refuge there after running away from Esau and his righteous wrath."

"Yes," I said. "Laban took you in when you really had nowhere to go, and you basically took what you could out of the relationship, didn't you?"

"Well…yes and no. Because of the kind of person Laban was, I had to exploit the situation at least as much as he did if I was going to survive. But I did not go there intending to turn the situation to my own advantage. What you do not understand is that my Uncle Laban was much worse than I could ever be! I very soon realized that if I allowed him to get the better of me, he would use me in every way he could. Everything Laban did was for Laban.

"You already know that I fell in love with his daughter Rachel the first time I saw her, that day at the well on the edge of Laban's territory. So what does he do? I ask him for her hand in marriage, he gives it, and then the old scoundrel tells me that first I have to work for him for seven years. And I do, because I am head over heels in love with her. So the time comes for the wedding. Everyone has a wonderful time, including me, until I wake up in bed the next morning and I find myself married to Rachel's older sister, Leah!

"So then I go to have it out with her old man, who is just as cool as he can be. Seems he forgot to tell me that because of local custom, the older daughter has to marry first. So I can have Rachel, too, he says, but I have to work for him for another seven years! Rachel and I were married a week later—at least I didn't have to wait while I did those other seven years of forced labor."

"Why did you stay? Did you give him your word of honor?" I asked dryly.

"No, I did not. I didn't have the cash to leave. In those days, as you know, cash meant land and animals. Anyway, I knew that it would be worth my while staying with Laban. He had things to teach me: after all, he was exactly what I longed to be, very successful and very rich. At that stage in my life that's exactly what I wanted from life."

I wanted to hear about other things. "But as I read Genesis, I get the feeling that as the years passed you began to want something else."

"Not yet. But around that time I began to see that no matter how much I had (and by this time I had quite a bit), I always wanted more, a lot more! I also began to notice that I was finding it harder to get along, to cut a few corners if I had to, without feeling any pain."

"Conscience?"

"Maybe, but it was more than that. I'd like to think I was growing up. I often would remember something that happened the time I first left home, thinking that Esau might kill me. The first night out, I dreamed that I was looking at a ladder between earth and heaven, with lots of figures moving up and down the rungs. I had a clear and strong sense of the presence of God, and God made me a promise. I can recall the words as if it was an hour ago: 'I am the LORD, the God of Abraham your father and the God of Isaac; the land on which you lie I will give to you and to your offspring...and all the families of the earth shall be blessed in you and in your offspring.'"

He looked at me as if he was afraid I might laugh at him. "All I can really tell you is that when I woke up, I felt pretty strange. I had the feeling that God had some plans for me and I wasn't going to like them very much! I have to admit that the dream didn't have much effect on how I behaved in the years following, but the odd feeling it gave me never left me. The memory of it would rise up from time to time, as if someone was calling to me. I now realize God was not so much calling the Jacob I was at that time—how can I put this?—but the Jacob that God wanted me to be. The real Jacob."

He shook his head. "Yes, I know. Sounds pretty bizarre. And I never forgot what I did to Esau. As you know, we were not only brothers, we were twins. Maybe you can never walk away from that, even though in our case we could not have been more different. Remember, I was much smaller than he was, much less athletic. Even though I made up for it by being smarter, Esau was the one our dad really liked."

He got out of his chair and went to the window. "In all those years we spent apart, I never stopped thinking about my brother. As I got older I began to see that he was everything I was not, that we were halves of a single self. I knew I had to find him. I dreaded it but I knew I had to do it. You know where the Bible says that I sent messengers before me to my brother Esau in the land of Seir? Notice that it says categorically that I initiated the meeting between us. At least I get the credit for that." I thought I detected a quick flash of resentment.

"So we headed the caravan south until the day one of my scouts rode in to tell me that Esau was in the area. It had me pretty nervous to hear that he had a large force of men with him; I could tell he was out to get even for the way I cheated him. I remember my whole life seemed to shrink before that guilt and—okay, I admit it!—my fear. For a few hours everything I had ever done seemed stupid and pointless, even marrying Rachel, whom I loved more than anything or anybody in the world."

I found myself beginning to like this brash, outspoken young man who seemed to know himself so well. "So that's why you decided to stay alone that night in the gorge of the Jabbock River?"

He smiled. "That's why. Though I must admit a few other possibilities popped into my head—like turning the whole caravan around and heading north into the mountains of the upper Galilee until Esau gave up on me!"

"And then you had another dream."

"Yes," he said, "and in that dream someone came to me. Maybe it was God, maybe some demon, maybe it was a part of myself I had never faced before, but whoever or whatever it was, we struggled. That part I'm certain about. Whoever or whatever struggled with me was from God. After what seemed hours, I knew in some mysterious way that I had won." He laughed. "I swear to you, I've never been so exhausted in my life! I literally limped away from that struggle, but at least I knew that I was limping into a new chapter of my life. I also knew that the first thing that would happen in this new chapter would be meeting my brother. The dream didn't take away my dread of that meeting."

"So you were just as afraid?"

"Of course. But the dream gave me the certainty that this is what I had to do if I wasn't going to keep running for the rest of my life."

"So you pulled all the stops out. Set up an elaborate display of all your possessions to impress Esau."

He reddened a little. "Just think for a minute what it was like to be me, about to meet someone you had been terrible to years ago. And not just anybody, but your own brother. You've avoided it for years. Both of you have grown, changed, lived your own lives. You don't know what to expect: all you know is that it's about to happen and you can't avoid it any more. And since this brother of yours is now an unknown quantity, you have no idea what he intends to do, but you do know he has a small army with him. Be honest—what would you do?"

"When you two did meet, how did you feel?"

He held up a hand. "Hang on! We're not there yet. There's more. When you haven't met since childhood you tend to think of the relationship as if it's still on those terms. I told you that Esau had always been bigger, louder, stronger. He laughed a lot, rode well, fought well, all the things I could never do. Sure, I was always smarter, and now I was richer, too. But the fact that my brother was about to come over the hill into my life again made me feel that I had achieved nothing, that inside I was still a kid."

"So you decided to send the caravans ahead to impress him?"

Jacob shrugged. "I did. I wasn't going to apologize for what I had achieved."

"So even if *you* couldn't impress Esau, your goods and chattels would. So what finally happened? Was he impressed?"

I was moved by the way he suddenly changed. Jacob had been on his feet all this time, sometimes addressing his replies to me, sometimes to the grounds outside. He came back, sat down, leaned forward towards me. His voice came alive, his whole expression eager. He put down the dregs of his drink and held out his arms. "Esau gave me a great bear hug that nearly broke my ribs! He just about lifted me off the ground." Suddenly he was laughing, shaking his head.

"And you?"

"Me? I didn't know what to do. My brother took me completely be surprise. I tried to tell him how much it meant to see him again."

"Is that all you said? Is that how you really felt?"

"Are you kidding? How I really felt was beyond words. When he gave me that bear hug and looked straight at me, I realized for the first time how big the hole in my life had been. Now that he was there and we finally met up, I think I tasted pure joy for a few moments. It was like daybreak—like being born all over again, weird as it sounds."

His face turned away from me as he tried to take hold of his emotions. We said nothing for a short time, and then I risked one more question. "Isn't it interesting that the meeting meant so much, yet the two of you still went your separate ways soon after?"

He nodded. "Life's like that. Typical Esau, he was all for my taking my whole household south to his people in Edom. Once again, I was the realist. I knew it wouldn't work. It had been wonderful to meet again, but the real point of our meeting was the reconciliation, nothing else. We still had to face the fact that we were poles apart in almost everything and we would never live in peace together. I saw this immediately and I suspect that deep down Esau knew it, too. When I turned our caravan west and stopped following his, he made no attempt to change my mind. He just continued down south."

"You never met again, did you?"

"Only once, when our father died. The whole extended family gathered in Hebron for the burial rites. It was good to meet again, but after things were over we said our farewells and life went on."

Suddenly there was nothing more to say. I don't know how long we sat there in silence until my friend once again became the wedding guest. Turning his head to look inside the big reception room, he said, "I think I hear someone proposing a toast. Shall we go inside?"

I held him back for a moment. I wanted to know. "Rachel was always the one, wasn't she?" I asked him gently.

His eyes looked beyond me. "Rachel died before our father did. She died giving birth to our youngest. Yes, for me she was always the one. Now let's go drink to the bride."

Together we went in and stood at the back of the crowd listening to the timeless pleasantries of such an occasion. Jacob's picture of the meeting of the two brothers stayed with me. I found myself reflecting on the many ways God has of bringing us to terms with ourselves, showing us who we are and at the same time giving us enough grace to accept what we find and then get on with our lives. I couldn't help thinking that although Jacob ended up being one of the great patriarchs of the Bible, maybe it was Esau, in his honest, blundering way, who made it possible for his brilliant and resourceful brother to become the instrument of God.

I know he stayed for a while because I saw him raise his glass in a few toasts. Sometime later I looked around for him, but he had gone.

3

Deborah

The Judge

The Israelites again did what was evil in the sight of the LORD, after Ehud died. So the LORD sold them into the hand of King Jabin of Canaan, who reigned in Hazor; the commander of his army was Sisera, who lived in Harosheth-ha-goiim. Then the Israelites cried out to the LORD for help; for he had nine hundred chariots of iron, and had oppressed the Israelites cruelly twenty years.

At that time Deborah, a prophetess, wife of Lappidoth, was judging Israel. She used to sit under the palm of Deborah between Ramah and Bethel in the hill country of Ephraim; and the Israelites came up to her for judgment. She sent and summoned Barak son of Abinoam from Kedesh in Naphtali, and said to him, "The LORD, the God of Israel, commands you, 'Go, take posi-

tion at Mount Tabor, bringing ten thousand from
the tribe of Naphtali and the tribe of Zebulun. I
will draw out Sisera, the general of Jabin's army, to
meet you by the Wadi Kishon with his chariots and
his troops; and I will give him into your hand.'"

Barak said to her, "If you will go with me, I will go;
but if you will not go with me, I will not go."And
she said, "I will surely go with you."

(Judges 4:1-9)

I had always wanted to meet the woman who, as far as I
knew, was absolutely unique in the history of Israel.
Now I had my chance. She had approached me in the
main lecture hall at the University of Tel Aviv after a talk
she had given on the role of women in the modern Israeli
army. A new member of the faculty, she had already published widely in her field. Certainly the lecture had been
very easy to listen to; she was immensely enthusiastic,
even brilliant. When she walked up and greeted me I was
almost certain that I was meeting one of my old friends
from scripture, so I decided I would try my hunch.

"I think I know you as Deborah. Am I right?" If I had
been mistaken, it would only have sounded like a wrong
guess at a first name. But I wasn't.

"You certainly are!" she laughed. "Is it that obvious?
Maybe I should be more careful about how I come across
to people!"

And so it began, this encounter with a gifted and
forceful woman who would never hesitate for a moment
to credit a higher power for whatever successes and vic-
tories she had known. We seated ourselves in a small

comfortable alcove down the hallway from the lecture room, and I told her how much her story had always intrigued me.

"Because of my being a judge?" she asked.

"Yes. By the time I come across you in the story here"—I indicated the Bible sticking out of my overflowing briefcase—"you have obviously become a kind of resident oracle. You dispense personal advice, give guidance to tribal leaders about local administrative problems, solve moral dilemmas. The oracle at Delphi in Greece comes to mind and, by the way, she was also a woman."

"I don't think it is 'by the way' at all," she said. "No coincidence. I think women have that gift. In those days we called it judging—at least that is your translation of our word—and in a sense it was. I would frequently be asked to decide a family dispute, or an argument over land or an inheritance, but much of the time I was doing what you call counseling, suggesting a basis for some course of action.

"What you must always remember is that whatever wisdom and discernment skills I had were assumed to be a gift. Nobody thought that the intuition or the wisdom was mine, and neither did I. I was just a voice, an instrument of the Lord. The concept is somewhat foreign today," she said dryly.

"In a sense it is," I said, "but not because the idea of someone speaking with the voice of God is unknown to us. It isn't. The problem we have is distinguishing a genuinely inspired person, a prophet, from someone who is crazy and in need of help."

Deborah nodded. "I understand perfectly. Of course we had that problem, too, and we dealt with it not so differently from you. If someone is mentally ill, and not a genuine channel for God, there is almost always some manifestation of the illness: an urge to dominate everyone around them, or a total inability to accept any questioning, or an expression of acute anxiety. I think we always have to watch out for false prophets."

I could see why Deborah was a force to be reckoned with. She was a crystal-clear thinker and highly articulate.

"What is especially interesting about you is that something other than those particular gifts put you into the story forever."

"I see. You must be talking about the northern military campaign."

"Yes, I am. Tell me, how does a woman whose primary contribution to her community was a mixture of personal counseling, moral influence, and legal advice suddenly become a first-class military strategist?"

"I didn't. The trick was to be able to put my finger on someone who was."

"You mean Barak?"

"Right. Barak was a first-class soldier and someone the tribes trusted implicitly. He had proven himself very able in the kind of guerrilla war we were waging with Jabin."

I was confused. "Jabin?"

She smiled. "Maybe every society has some kind of threat from the outside that refuses to go away. Maybe every society needs one. Anyway, Jabin was ours—a local warlord who was determined to get rid of us.

"But back to Barak. One of the benefits of being a judge was that I was very well known, and I had developed a large network of friends and associates who could provide me with all kinds of intelligence sources. At that time we were gradually taking over the country, although we had not yet succeeded in overcoming the northern part—the Galilee. The main reason we wanted it was the Jezreel Valley. Not only is it the most luscious part of the country, it is also a main east-west passage. If you control Jezreel you have the heartland, which is exactly why the Canaanites had no intention of giving it up without a fight."

"So your troops decided to take it?"

"Yes, but there were other factors. It was not only that the Canaanites held the valley; if that was all, we would probably have tried to negotiate some kind of agreement for partial use. There was more than enough land for everyone. But north of the valley was the rest of the Galilee, which we knew was beautiful and ideal for settlement, especially around the lake. In addition, the Canaanite leader Jabin had been raiding southward and mounting terrorist attacks against us for years. He was never quite sure when we would mobilize and go after him, so he tried to keep us on edge by raiding. The time had come when we'd had enough."

"And that was when the tribal leaders came to you. Did they have a plan?"

"Of course not. Providing a plan was up to me—I was the one in the planning and advice business!"

"So how did you feel when they came to you?"

"Surprised. A little frightened, to tell the truth—at first, anyway. Then I began to think it through. I knew that we must not underestimate Jabin. He was clever, had good resources, and was well entrenched, not only in the valley but in the highlands north of it.

"So then I made two decisions. I called in Barak, who was the most competent military strategist we had in the

army. We had known each other a long time. Remember
that most of us in leadership roles had grown up together as children in the tribe. I told him I was convinced we
had to fight from a superior vantage point, which meant
we needed to get up higher than the valley floor. Barak
agreed, and persuaded me that the obvious choice was
Tabor, a small steep mountain on the north side of the
valley."

"Your idea was to weld the local tribes into a coalition.
That very nearly failed, didn't it?"

"Very nearly. Mainly because our people had never
joined together as tribes, at least not since coming out of
the desert. I knew I could depend on the tribes of
Naphtali and Dan because they were the nearest: they
stood to benefit immediately if we won the campaign
against Jabin. After they vowed their support, I succeeded in getting some help from Ephraim and Benjamin to
the south of us. The most pleasant surprise was the
arrival of a contingent from Manasseh, a surprise
because they lived east of the Jordan. The rest of the
tribes let us down with this or that excuse."

"I know. I've read what you said after it was all over.
You didn't mince words!"

She laughed. "I was so angry. Even our victory didn't
change how I felt. We could have lost everything just
because some key tribes stayed away. They couldn't see
that although they were far enough away to be reasonably safe, our struggle was their struggle, too."

Suddenly wanting to remember her exact words, I
pulled out the Bible and opened it up. "You and Barak
even sang the song of victory together."

"And we danced! Did we dance that day! Everybody
celebrated the victory."

I traced a finger down the pages. "Here we are. Here is where you list the tribes who failed to turn up on the battlefield: 'Among the clans of Reuben there were great searchings of heart. Why did you tarry among the sheepfolds, to hear the piping for the flocks?'"

I looked across at her. "Do I hear some heavy sarcasm?"

"You certainly do. They deserved every word of it."

I continued reading. "Gilead stayed beyond the Jordan; and Dan, why did he abide with the ships? Asher sat still at the coast of the sea, settling down by his landings."

She shook her head. "If I let myself, I could still get angry all over again remembering that!"

"Even if those tribes stayed away, you must have had about ten thousand troops."

"About that. Our storytellers tended to add a few more every time they told the story! But the most serious problem was what we did *not* have. We had no chariots, while our spies told us that Jabin had nearly a thousand. We had come to respect those chariots. They had beaten us again and again. Our hope this time was to beat down Jabin's forces by sheer force of numbers."

"And you did!"

"We did, but not just by our numbers. Jabin's commander Sisera and his troops started from the western end of the valley, the coast end. Because we had gone high up on the slopes of Mount Tabor, we could see them miles away."

"So you were actually there, up on the mountain with your people?"

"I had to be. The first thing Barak said to me was that he would plan the campaign only on the condition that I would be there with him, up on the heights, the day the battle took place."

"For Barak to say that to a woman must have been a little unusual. It shows how much trust he had in you."

"Barak was shrewd, and he knew that my being there would be good for morale. Many of the troops knew me: I had helped some with land and grazing problems, and others with family questions—inheritance and division of property. I think he also wanted someone who would share the responsibility (and the blame) in case things went wrong for us. Both of us knew that we were putting everything on the line that day. It was make or break with Jabin and his marauders, winner take all."

I was surprised. "It was that serious?"

"Yes," she said, "that serious. So you can imagine how I felt, watching close to a thousand chariots rolling towards us. All our infantry around me, crouching in the grass and the trees, were there because they trusted Barak and me. If I was proven wrong in the decision to face off with Jabin and his army, I would lose that trust forever."

"What about *you*? Usually there are reasons why we take a risk and place our life on the line. What made it possible for you to do that? It says in the story that you trusted in the Lord. What did that mean to you?"

"In your kind of language, perhaps a sense of destiny, or a sense that somehow it was the right thing to do and the right time. I felt the campaign against Jabin and the Canaanites was meant to be. We had come through so much to that point—not my generation, perhaps, but those before us. We had survived Egypt, crossed the Red Sea, journeyed through Sinai. In the years since then, we'd had our defeats and setbacks, our times of questioning God, but we had always managed to make gains. I knew without a doubt that this land was meant to be ours. Maybe the simplest way to put it is this: I had come to believe that somebody—and for me that somebody was the Lord—meant us to have it. That day on Tabor, watching the chariots coming towards us, I guess I believed that even if we lost that day, we would win some other time."

"Just suppose something," I said. "Suppose you had lost that day. Suppose that it hadn't rained, that the chariots had not bogged down. Suppose everything you loved and valued had been destroyed. Those of you who survived to rebuild the tribe—what would you have done?"

She didn't hesitate a moment. "We would have set about discovering what weaknesses and moral failures—what sins, if you like—had made it impossible for God to give us the victory. As individuals and as a nation, we would have begun rebuilding our relationship with God."

Her directness hit home: it both startled and refreshed me. I was silent. She could see the effect her words had had on me, and waited for me to rally. To give myself a little time, I took the Bible, still open at chapter five of the book of Judges, and pointed to verse twenty-one.

"You say here that the Lord did something you could never have planned."

"You mean the rain? I couldn't believe it. We had seen the clouds coming in from the west. It was obvious that we were in for a downpour, but what we had not factored in was a build-up from the rainy spring we had earlier that year. There was already a lot of water in the Galilee highlands, including on Mount Tabor itself. It was only when we heard the sound of the rising streams and gullies around us that we realized the possibilities. We could see the valley floor begin to soften as the water gathered. The chariots of those days were terribly heavy, and right away they began to bog down. No doubt about it: the Canaanites were in trouble. Barak gave the signal and our people poured down the hillside. Sisera's troops did not have a chance. It was all over in a couple of hours."

"You believe God sent the rain, don't you?"

"I do. I know that is difficult for someone living in the late twentieth century to grasp, but there you are. I believed it then and I still do."

"To be honest, I envy you that kind of trust in—in things."

Deborah smiled, obviously amused at this late-twentieth-century man, amused and a little sad. "There you go again," she said. "What do you mean by my 'trust in things'? Why don't you just say God?"

"I don't know," I said ruefully. It was my turn to be sad. The sadness remained even after our conversation came to a close and she left to teach a seminar on the other side of the campus. In the days that followed, I found myself longing for her quality of trust.

~❦

4

Delilah

The Spy

After this he fell in love with a woman in the valley
of Sorek, whose name was Delilah. The lords of the
Philistines came to her and said to her, "Coax him,
and find out what makes his strength so great, and
how we may overpower him, so that we may bind
him in order to subdue him; and we will each give
you eleven hundred pieces of silver."

So Delilah said to Samson, "Please tell me what
makes your strength so great, and how you could
be bound, so that one could subdue you."

(Judges 16:4-6)

We had met in one of the loveliest and, as far as I
know, least visited parts of Israel. If you drive
southwest from Jerusalem, taking the highway towards

Tel Aviv on the coast, you come to a turnoff on the left for Beth Shemesh. Eventually you find yourself in a prosperous hillside town, partly industrialized, overlooking what was known long ago as the valley of Sorek.

Drive through the town to the small national park and you come to an intricate system of caves. Today its entrance includes a tiny theater in which you see a video about the area, and then you begin the marvelous journey into the recesses of the cave, its age-old stalagmites and stalactites glistening in the shadows like the pillars of some ancient cathedral.

I had encountered the woman first as our guide. Very pleasant and good at her job, she readily shared information as we moved down through the galleries of the cave and worked our way upward again. Afterward, as we were lined up for lunch at the cafeteria attached to the park, she invited me to share a small table on the balcony. Stretching her hand towards me in order to introduce herself and speaking with a slight accent, she said, "I think you know me as Delilah."

After expressing my delight, I confessed to her that from the moment she had told us the name of the valley below the town I had begun to think of Samson, but it had never occurred to me that she and I would meet.

"I understand," she assured me. "The place is full of his memory. Even the name of today's town, Beth Shemesh, shares the same root as the name Samson. He's everywhere here."

"Do you mind if I ask you a few things about him?"

"Not at all," she smiled, still very much a hospitable guide. "Ask whatever you wish. I'll try to be helpful."

"Forgive my putting it this way," I said, "but I think Samson always puzzles people because they can't decide

whether he was something of a clown, or a real hero." I put
the question so bluntly because I sensed even at this early
stage that Delilah was prepared to be equally objective.

"It depends on your point of view," she replied. "In
Samson's time this area belonged to the tribe of Dan,
although they gave up trying to farm it and most of them
moved northeast to the foothills around Mount Hermon.
But if you were an Israelite of that tribe in this hill country, Samson was most certainly a hero."

"Hero, yes, but *judge?* I think many people who have
heard or read the stories of Israel in the days of the
judges find it strange that this character was a judge over
Israel alongside figures like Deborah and Gideon. It
doesn't seem to fit."

She thought for a moment before speaking. "I think
that you are being misled by contemporary ideas of what
it means to judge. The reality then was completely different: judges were charismatic military leaders whom
the Israelites followed to victory, like Deborah against the
Canaanites and Gideon against the Midianites. And it
won't help to think in national terms, because there was
no such thing as the nation of Israel, just tribes scattered
over various areas—Dan here, Judah there."

As we stood on the balcony, she waved her hand
towards the stretch of countryside that fell away to the
west. "I've already mentioned that this was the area of the
tribe of Dan. Not far away was the tribe of Judah. They
come into the story, but let's come back to that later."

"Are you saying that a judge could be any man or
woman who was recognized by the tribe, or a local con-
federation of tribes, as being an outstanding leader?" I
asked.

"Yes, but that isn't all. It had to be clear that the chosen person had a special relationship with God. It is essential to remember this, especially when you and others wonder how someone like Samson could have been a judge. You're absolutely right in saying that he was more of an adventurer and a warrior than a strategist, yet he was also someone that his people could believe in."

"I sometimes think that Samson was playing the role that some media figures play today," I replied, "larger than life, embodying strengths that nine out of ten people could only dream of, always attacking the bad guys and getting away with it. In his day, you Philistines were certainly the bad guys!"

"You could say that," she said. "Samson's people were afraid of us and so naturally they hated us. To hear of him harassing us and getting away with it was music to their ears. Our leaders knew they had to deal directly with him, or their domination of the local Israelite tribes would begin to slip."

"To your people, then, he was not just a nuisance. He was a real threat. Am I right?"

"Yes and no," she replied. "For a while we saw him as nothing more than a dangerous bully. Then we came to realize that it would be very stupid and risky to underestimate him. Even so," she smiled, "that doesn't change the fact that he was a bully—though a very smart and powerful one."

"What intrigues me about this whole story," I said, "is how badly the Israelites seemed to need a hero at that time. I think of them as being able to handle almost anything, yet somehow your people seemed to be a kind of nemesis for them. Almost as if the very name Philistine made them lose their nerve."

She nodded. "I think that's true, at least in part. Why this came to be is anyone's guess. My own explanation is that the Israelites were essentially a land people and we had been a sea people for a long time, so to them it was as though we came from a different planet. We were so unlike their other enemies, or maybe we just didn't react in ways they had come to expect. After a battle you would often hear our men expressing surprise at how unpredictable the Israelites were in the field; it shook their confidence. Small wonder, then, that when this Samson comes along, the whole tribe cheers his exploits, and mothers begin to put their children to bed with stories about him."

I thought I heard a note of grudging admiration in her voice. She struck me as someone secure enough in herself to admit this freely. Clearly, she was not a person with a cause. There was no sign of a wish to attack. I instinctively liked her, and that made me realize how much her very name has been a strike against her, always associated with the seductive temptress who betrays Samson to his enemies.

"The stories about him," I asked, "have they been exaggerated?"

"Oh dear, yes," she replied. "But then everything tends to be exaggerated when it is turned into story and legend. Look at television! What about the movies you go to—do they exaggerate any less than we did?"

I laughed. "Touché. We have Samsons all over the place. Superheroes, larger than life, blowing things up, killing off the forces of evil, saving the world."

"Exactly," she replied. "That was Samson. Just try being surrounded by a thousand armed men, your only weapon the jawbone of an ass, and see how long *you* last.

But, as we both know, it makes a great campfire story. There's a story in your book of Judges where Samson ties together pairs of foxes by their tails, sticks a blazing torch in the knotted tails, and sends them into our cornfields just before harvest time. I admit it shows an imaginative touch, and it did a lot of harm at a crucial time of year, but three hundred foxes? Let's settle for a dozen, shall we? That would have been enough to wreak havoc."

"The strange thing," I said, "was that he had this ongoing war with your people, but he kept on getting involved with Philistine women. Wouldn't you say that's a little perverse?"

She shook her head. "Not a bit, if you knew Samson. Or maybe I should say, if you knew him from a woman's point of view. He tended to seek out Philistine women and he found them in the whorehouses of Gaza. What women found when he showed interest in them was that, above all, he needed to dominate them."

"He certainly didn't dominate you."

Immediately I wished I could take back what I said. Her next words had an air of deliberate patience about them. "I came as the last of a number of women in Samson's life, and by that time it was widely known what Samson was. Anyway," she shrugged, "I only came into the picture as an agent fulfilling a contract. I was hired to be there—I cared nothing for him."

"Samson married fairly early in life, didn't he?" I enquired.

"Yes," she said. "That was the first sign of his interest in our women. His family tried to stop him but he insisted. She was a girl from Timnah. Samson's family lived in Zorah, only a few miles away but higher up the valley. Come to think of it, maybe that was partly the reason for his lifelong struggle with us. I sometimes think that a tragic thing was going on within Samson. He lived so near to us, yet could never be part of us. We Philistines were bigger, richer, stronger than his tribe of Dan. These were all the things he wanted to be."

I decided to backtrack for a while. "There is something about Samson's early marriage that has always intrigued me. The Bible says that he goes to Timnah, sees a Philistine woman, and decides he wants her. He comes home and orders—certainly he doesn't ask—his parents to get her for him. That's exactly the expression he uses. The parents remonstrate with him about marrying outside the tribe. It makes no difference. Samson insists. His words have a remarkable selfishness and lack of feeling: 'Get her for me, because she pleases me!'

"But right in the next breath, here is what the storyteller says: 'His father and mother did not know that this was from the LORD; for he was seeking a pretext to act against the Philistines.' That's the part that has me puzzled. Here is a grown man bullying his parents to 'get' this woman who 'pleases' him, flying in the face of every tradition they know, letting his tribe down, and suddenly he becomes the instrument of God's will for his people. What's going on here?"

For the first time, she seemed almost angry. "What's going on is something rather hard for you to understand, coming as you do from the modern west. Forgive me for putting it like this, but why should anyone who is an instrument of God for others have to be a pillar of the community, a respectable citizen who sings in the church choir? Given what people are, candidates would be in very short supply! When you really think about it, you know as well as I do that God chooses the particular person needed to fulfill his purposes, despite our qualms!"

I became very quiet, feeling I had been put in my place for my shallow judgments. I realized she had been right to take me to task. I said as much, and she nodded graciously at my apology.

"Take the question that always revolves around Samson's long hair," she said. "Whenever the story is told, my role is recounted in great detail: the temptress who destroyed him by worming his secret out of him."

"You mean you didn't have a hand in destroying him?"

She gave a long sigh, as if worn out by trying to get across her point of view. "Try to see the situation as we saw it in Gaza," she said. "Here was this man, something of a nuisance, who gradually encouraged his whole people to fear us less, and therefore possibly to challenge us."

"That is why you were paid so much to trap him?"

There was no apology in her voice. "Yes, that is why I was paid so much money to trap him. I made myself expensive. Why not? If things had gone wrong, it would have cost me my life. What I dislike so much is the way in which the whole incident has been passed on."

"Are you saying that it was different from the Bible record?"

"Yes and no. Yes, in the sense that I *did* ask Samson the secret of his strength many times, and we even joked about it. But at the same time, no, not in the sense that his long hair was in some magical way the source of his strength. To take that message from the story is to trivialize it."

She leaned forward for emphasis. "The fact is that I think I met the real Samson in the last few minutes we ever saw each other."

"The real Samson? What do you mean?"

"I mean that you should listen much more carefully to the reply he gave me when I asked him for the third time to tell me the source of his great strength. I shall always remember what he said and the way he said it. He spoke very quietly and deliberately. I knew he was revealing himself to me in a way he had probably never revealed himself to anybody else. He said to me, 'A razor has never come upon my head; for I have been a nazirite to God from my mother's womb. If my head were shaved, then my strength would leave me; I would become weak, and be like anyone else.' That is what he said."

I was genuinely puzzled. "I still don't understand."

"I know you don't," she said resignedly, "nor has anyone else. Don't you see that the important words for Samson were *a nazirite to God*? That identity is what drove him and gave him what he referred to as his strength. Yes, he was strong, immensely so. Yes, he was sexually driven. Yes, he had a kind of obsession about the Philistines. But beneath all of these drives, and deeper than any of them, was a man who truly saw himself as, in some sense, the hand of God. That was the source of his strength. The long hair was a *symbol* of that strength, but only because it was a mark of his dedication."

I thought for a moment. "But if that was truly so, why should the cutting of his hair have made him give up, as he seems to have done? After all, it would grow back again. Come to think of it, the Bible says that it began to grow again in captivity."

She thought for a moment. "I can't really give you an answer. I can only try to guess at one. I think there were at least three Samsons, all driving him and stoking up this tremendous energy: let's call them the man of God, the terrorist, and the lover. By the time he and I met, I think all his circuits were ready to blow. He was running out of the energy he needed to live out all the roles. In the end he was a terrorist both in his own eyes and, later on, in the eyes of his people—God's terrorist."

"He literally brought the roof down," I said.

"Yes," she said, smiling sadly. "Within himself that must have been a supreme moment. Think of it. All the struggle is over, everything resolved. With your last breath you wreak havoc on the people you hate most in the world, and you know it will make all the difference for your own people."

For a while there was silence. I broke it because I felt genuinely grateful and I wanted her to know it. "Remember earlier when I said I couldn't see how his people could ever have given him the honor of being a judge in Israel?"

"Yes," she said, waiting.

"I now understand, thanks to you. They gave him the honor of being judge in Israel because they saw what *you* came to see in those last few hours, and what I have never seen, at least until now. They saw that Samson was above all a man of God."

"I am absolutely sure of it," she said as we finished our lunch and took leave of one another.

5

Ruth

The Refugee

In the days when the judges ruled, there was a famine in the land, and a certain man of Bethlehem in Judah went to live in the country of Moab, he and his wife and two sons. The name of the man was Elimelech and the name of his wife Naomi, and the names of his two sons were Mahlon and Chilion; they were Ephrathites from Bethlehem in Judah. They went into the country of Moab and remained there.

But Elimelech, the husband of Naomi, died, and she was left with her two sons. These took Moabite wives; the name of the one was Orpah and the name of the other Ruth. When they had lived there about ten years, both Mahlon and Chilion also died, so that the woman was left without her two sons and her husband.

Then she started to return with her daughters-in-law from the country of Moab, for she had heard in the country of Moab that the LORD had considered his people [in Judah] and given them food. So she set out from the place where she had been living, she and her two daughters-in-law, and they went on their way to go back to the land of Judah.

(Ruth 1:1-7)

One of the facts of life today in any great city is the presence of an enormous flow of immigrants. Sometimes the people arriving are educated, eager, and able to carve out their own niche in a new country; others—and they are the majority—possess little more than what they can carry in suitcases. Quite often the latter are refugees seeking asylum from persecution or war. These are the people and the circumstances that bring the churches, especially inner-city churches, into the picture.

Over the years my particular church congregation has sponsored a number of immigrants, both individuals and families. Because we developed a reasonable degree of expertise in this area, a number of our members became involved in immigration work at local border crossings, the airport, and a few downtown reception areas. And, as any priest would, I wished to give support to those who had made a serious commitment to a form of ministry that at times can be demanding.

So it was that I found myself at a regional conference of agencies who shoulder responsibility for various aspects of immigration outreach. After a keynote address, we all moved into workshops. As the morning proceeded I noticed one woman in the large group who asked very insightful questions. She seemed to have an inside knowledge of the problems facing displaced people. Whenever she spoke she was listened to, yet she never dominated the discussion or tried to take over direction of the group.

At the coffee break I made a point of introducing myself and thanking her. A number of people were doing the same thing, and I had expected to be no more than one of these, saying my thanks, receiving her pleasant smile of appreciation, and moving on. To my surprise, when the cluster of people around her had cleared, she came over in my direction, obviously wishing to talk further. "Have you a little time on your hands?" she asked. "I would very much like to chat for a while. You and I may have more in common than you realize."

I had no idea of what we might have in common. The refugee and immigration work, of course, but somehow I knew she meant more than this. I assured her that I had made no other commitments for the morning. She in turn suggested that we might sit out the second half of the workshop and find somewhere to talk, which is exactly what we proceeded to do.

For a short while we talked about the morning, the mood of the conference, her hopes for the work ahead in the city. Then she said, "You must be wondering what other things we have in common." I admitted to being curious.

"The answer is, a book. Or a chapter within a book."

I was immediately alert to a wonderful possibility, that someone was once again about to step from the world of the Bible into my time and world. I still had not figured out her identity, and my bewilderment must have showed.

"You know me as Ruth," she said.

So began our time together. As with all the men and women I have encountered in this way, I had the peculiar feeling of both knowing them and yet not knowing them. I mentioned this to Ruth: "I feel I have known you since I've been a child, yet meeting you like this makes it all so completely different."

She nodded. "I feel the same way. Being able to tell one's story first-hand is immensely satisfying. I know that you know the story, yet you don't know *me*—and that makes all the difference."

"Whenever I read your story I always think of you as being in charge, even in situations where you were extremely vulnerable."

"Thank you," she replied, "but that is only how it looks from the outside. Believe me, I didn't always feel that way! I had times of abject fear, even moments of terror when I wondered if I could go on. But most of the time, given the realities of life for me then, I didn't have a choice. I just had to keep going."

Sometimes I look at people who have come through great tribulation and I marvel at them. I looked at Ruth and saw the strength in her face, the calmness and self-possession in her eyes and in her voice. What a privilege it was to meet her. A memory surfaced of a special moment I wanted to share with her.

"A particular place I have visited a number of times always makes me think of you. It is a kind of pull-out area on the road that goes down to the Jordan valley from Jerusalem. If you stand there, you can see a long way east into Jordan and southeast into what would have been Moab in your time. I have often imagined seeing the tiny figures of the three of you walking along the way: you, your sister-in-law Orpah, and your mother-in-law Naomi. I imagine you as tiny dark figures against the desert, approaching the Jordan, trying to find a ford to cross, but first having your discussion about who would cross and who would go back east."

"The choice of returning to Moab with Orpah wasn't really a choice for me," she replied. "First of all, it was terribly risky to go back. I have often wondered what happened to my sister-in-law, a solitary woman in the desert. We never heard from her again. But for me there was something else, and that was Naomi. The simple fact was that I had come to love my mother-in-law very much."

"God knows you had been through enough together."

"Yes, we had. But she had been through even more. Just think of it. There she is, happily married and living in the area around Bethlehem, among her own people, with a husband who loves her, two small boys she adores, and suddenly her universe caves in. Famine hits hard. They face starvation. To get away from it they have to leave a reasonably pleasant area and head southeast into much harsher countryside. Presumably they know nobody, so they are exiles and strangers as well.

"Naomi does all this, and she makes a home for them somehow. Then the ultimate disaster hits. Her husband dies. She survives this, enjoys seeing the marriages of her sons to local women, hopes again for the future. Next her two sons die—not one, but two. And there she is. No longer youthful, left with two young daughters-in-law, all three of us widows—the most vulnerable and fragile situation one can imagine in that world.

"The point I'm trying to make is that she came through this ordeal magnificently, always thinking of us before herself, loving us as if we had been her own. It was she who decided to make the long journey north and west back to her people. Look at a map some day and see what that journey was like. There were times when we thought we would never make it."

"Was it Naomi who invited you two to come with her?"

"We insisted. There was no way she could do it on her own. We postponed deciding whether or not we would accompany her all the way to the area around Bethlehem and the land holdings of her extended family. One alternative we had was to get her to the Jordan and see her across somehow; then she would be safe. Even this worried us because that last part of the Jordan valley, from the river crossing up the escarpment to Bethlehem, involves a steep and long climb up through terrain that is mostly bare rock face or scrub, at least at that time of the year."

"So in the end, the two sisters-in-law had to decide what to do. You arrived at the Jordan. Had you already made up your mind?"

"I had no doubt that I was going to stay with Naomi. She was my dear friend, and in a real sense, she had become a mother to me. I knew I was taking a risk going with her. Daughter-in-law or not, I would always be a foreigner in her country and among her people. At the time I gave no thought to the possibility of marrying again."

"In the book that is named after you, it says that the two of you came to Bethlehem at the beginning of the barley harvest. I have always felt it was a wonderful contrast to the way in which poor Naomi first set out: she left with her family in the midst of a famine, and returned with you in a time of golden harvest."

She nodded. "And it *was* golden. After the starkness of Moab, I thought I was in heaven. And this very harvest was a means of getting some food for us by my going into the fields and gleaning behind the reapers, picking up what had been discarded or overlooked. It was the law at that time. The poor could gather what the reapers had left behind."

"Then, you struck it lucky."

Her face broke into a smile. "Boaz. Yes, I suppose it was pure luck he decided to come out to the fields and check on the harvesters that day. When I saw him coming towards me I was terrified he was going to tell me to clear off. Remember, I was not one of his tribe or extended family, relationships that meant everything in that world. Instead, he was kindness itself. He suggested I work nearer to the reapers and gave instructions that I was not to be harassed by the male workers."

"I suspect that a grim reality lay behind that advice."

"In truth, there was. Again, remember I was a refugee as well as a woman. Without protection I was absolutely vulnerable. That was the greatest gift Boaz could have given me."

"Did you suspect any other intentions from him that day?"

"None at all. Looking back, it would be unthinkable for him to be interested in me beyond doing a kindness for a foreign daughter-in-law of Naomi. I even asked him why he was doing this for me. As it turns out, he had heard that I had been a help to Naomi on the journey. Obviously he had a great deal of respect for my mother-in-law."

"But later on, when the reapers all broke for a meal, he shared his meal with you, didn't he? Did that not alert you to something going on?"

"Again, no, because, as I said, it would be incredible under the circumstances. Remember that I did not know who Boaz was until I got home that first evening and Naomi put two and two together. She told me that Boaz was related in some way to Mahlon, my dead husband."

I smiled. "Naomi was quick to see the possibilities of that relationship. Did her suggestion startle you?"

"That I make up my face, put on my best clothes, and choose a moment when Boaz was alone?"

"Yes. To say the least, it was a direct approach! If Boaz had misinterpreted your action, it could have been disastrous."

Again she smiled, this time conspiratorially. "I suspect you're right. Let's just say that Naomi knew her man better than I did, because it did work. Not that anything happened between us that night. Boaz was concerned about the fact that there was another landowner who was even nearer to Naomi as kinsman than he. In those days, if the head of a household died, the next of kin would buy his property and become guardian and protector of his survivors. Boaz also showed real kindness in taking care that I not be seen leaving the place where we had spent the night."

"So this other landowner could have rightfully bought not just Naomi's husband's property, but also the rights to you and Naomi?"

"Yes. That probably sounds primitive to you, but in those days it was the custom."

"As things turned out, the other man declined to take over the property. You were lucky."

"True, I was lucky, but I don't really think it was just luck. You moderns seem to have difficulty believing that God has a hand in the way life goes."

"We do a lot of wrestling with that," I said, "but the truth is that we don't really know what to believe." Wishing to avoid a long discussion, I added, "So you and Boaz were married."

"Yes. And this will sound strange to you, but the joy I felt was not just for myself. I had immense respect for this man, and it rapidly grew into love, but part of my joy was for Naomi. She had been through so much. It was wonderful to be able to give her back some pleasure in life, especially now that she was getting on in years. I think my most joyful moment was when I was able to offer our first child to Naomi to hold. She was ecstatic. The other women sensed the joy of this moment. One of them called out, 'A son has been born to Naomi.' I felt like hugging that woman. The sight of Naomi with our child made up for all that had happened to us both over the years."

"So that moment of celebration was really the high point for you?" I asked.

"What do you mean?" She was obviously puzzled.

"You do know what comes after that in the story, don't you?"

She relaxed. "Oh, I see what you're referring to—the fact that our little son turned out to be the grandfather of David."

"Exactly. That's pretty significant, don't you think? Here you are, refugee turned into matriarch—the mother of kings!"

"How grand you make it sound. But none of that was in our minds the day Naomi first took my child Obed in her arms, and Boaz and I looked on."

I was very moved, although I wasn't sure why. I had to think for a moment. "What you've just said shows what kind of person you are."

"What do you mean?" she asked.

"You mention everyone else before you mention yourself."

"I don't know what to say to that."

"You don't have to say anything."

Realizing that I had embarrassed her slightly, I quickly changed the direction of our conversation.

"I want to ask you something about the book as we have it in our Bible. It seems to me that the main reason your book was kept among the scrolls and eventually became part of scripture is the fact we just acknowledged: from you and Boaz a king was born. Not just any king but David the king, the greatest king in Israel. But in our day this particular significance doesn't loom as large. It isn't part of our western perspective, so we tend to be left with an engaging love story that has a wonderfully happy ending."

She smiled, nodding her head.

"Don't feel I'm belittling your story by saying that," I continued. "It's just that I wonder if you have any thoughts about how the book of Ruth could speak to us more immediately. What meaning does it have for us at the end of the twentieth century?"

To my surprise, there was no hesitation in her reply. "I would have brought this up even if you had not," she began. "I particularly wanted to get in touch with you in the context of this workshop, in light of the refugee work you are involved in. I think your best use of my story is to link it with the vast migrations that are happening in your own time. Borders are being invaded everywhere and this isn't going to stop. I have a feeling that the work that you and others are doing is only beginning."

She leaned forward to emphasize what she was saying. "Use me as a figure in that work. In modern terms, I was a refugee. All three of us were refugees that day we made our decisions on the banks of the Jordan. And what happened to us? Naomi and I found a community—and not just a community, but a welcome. That is what made all the difference. It could have been so different. You know from your history how utterly vulnerable a solitary woman was in that world. The welcome of the community, the kindness of Boaz, made all the difference."

She glanced at her watch and stood, but continued to talk quickly and urgently. "Use my story as a call to welcome immigrants into your society. Use the figure of Boaz to speak to leaders who are in a position to be of immense assistance if only they choose to be. And Orpah's unknown fate can serve as a reminder of the many refugees at risk in an unfamiliar culture. That's how my story can be useful to you and to this work. Excuse the long reply but, as I said, this is the real reason I decided to make contact with you."

She extended a hand. I took it, held it for a moment. "Thank you more than I say. I will share your story." She acknowledged my thanks, smiled, and left.

6

Michal

The King's Daughter

So David went and brought up the ark of God from the house of Obed-edom to the city of David with rejoicing; and when those who bore the ark of the Lord had gone six paces, he sacrificed an ox and a fatling. David danced before the Lord with all his might; David was girded with a linen ephod....

As the ark of the Lord came into the city of David, Michal daughter of Saul looked out of the window, and saw King David leaping and dancing before the Lord; and she despised him in her heart....

David returned to bless his household. But Michal the daughter of Saul came out to meet David, and said, "How the king of Israel honored himself today, uncovering himself today before the eyes of his servants' maids, as any vulgar fellow might shamelessly uncover himself!" David said to Michal, "It was before the LORD, who chose me in place of your father and all his household, to appoint me as prince over Israel, the people of the LORD, that I have danced before the LORD."

(2 Samuel 6:12-16, 20-21)

We had been together for only half an hour and I was tired already. Not tired of her company, but simply of her energy: she exuded so much vitality and life that I felt I could never keep up with her. She had appeared in my office and introduced herself as the owner of a women's fashion boutique near the cathedral. She explained that she was organizing a function for her special customers, and needed a space downtown.

When we first met, the furthest thing from my mind was that I might be encountering one of my visitors from scripture. It happened very simply. I had excused myself from the office to check with one of the staff about the availability of a space. I walked in five minutes later to see her putting down the Bible that had been on my desk. My eyes must have registered something because there was a silence, as if she was making up her mind what to say.

"My name is Michal," she said as she gave me a broad smile.

For a moment my mind went blank and I searched desperately to remember who she was. Thank heaven I figured it out quickly; otherwise, I would have hurt her feelings. However, I still put my foot in my mouth. "David's Michal?" I asked brightly.

This was my first mistake. She rolled her eyes. "How like a man. I wasn't David's Michal. I wasn't anybody's Michal. I was my own Michal!"

"Sorry. I didn't mean it that way. It was just—"

"Just that David overshadows everyone else in the book, just as he overshadowed everyone around him in real life."

"Did he?"

"You know very well he did!"

There was a directness about her that invited the same kind of response. "How is it that you seemed to spend your whole life with men who overshadowed everyone around them? How could you put up with those huge egos?"

"Who else do you mean, other than David?"

"Your father, the king. Saul. Wasn't he bigger than life, just like David?"

She laughed. "Well, come to think of it, yes! But your theory is too neat. It doesn't apply to all the men in my life. When the relationship between my father and David completely fell apart, to the point where David couldn't appear anywhere within the king's domain, my father decided he was going to get the best of him. David and I had been married for quite some time, but out of sheer spite my father married me off to this pathetic minor supporter of his, Paltiel. Nothing defines Paltiel better than his response when David eventually came to power and demanded I come back to his household."

"What happened?"

"David literally sent in the troops. It was so typical. He marched into the house, ignored poor old Paltiel, told me I had a few minutes to pack. Paltiel followed behind almost the whole way, keeping his distance, crying and wailing like a child. I felt sorry for him, and at the same time deeply ashamed. He was timid and dull, but he had been kind to me."

"You were one of five children, weren't you? Three brothers, an older sister, and then you. I suppose it wasn't easy carving out a place in the family. I have a hunch you spent your life trying to carve out a place for yourself among others you always thought were bigger, stronger, and smarter."

"You're quite the family therapist, aren't you? But that's not so far from the truth."

"One thing that's obvious is that you were head over heels in love with David from early on."

"Yes and no. Remember that the story you know was written long after we had finished with all our loving and our hating. And it was written by a historian whose job was to put David and his entire reign in the best possible light. Life is never quite as neat as the stories people tell about it later, is it?"

"But you *were* in love with him?"

"If you insist. Yes, I was. Although perhaps it's truer to say that there was a time I was in love with David."

I suddenly felt that I was being far too inquisitive, so I back-tracked and went another way. I had always been fascinated by the personality of her father, Saul, and this seemed a good time to find out more.

"Looking back, knowing what you know now, what about the other powerful man in your life? Did you think that your father was going out of his mind?"

"I don't think so. With one exception, he handled things reasonably well all the way through his reign. The exception, of course, was David. Right from the beginning the relationship was intense and even violent. One moment he would treat David like his long-lost son, and the next he would be conspiring to kill him. At one point, my father even tried to enlist my brother Jonathan in his plan to kill David."

"But the very fact that he approached Jonathan at all tells you that he wasn't able to think clearly when it came to David. Jonathan was the last person who would choose to conspire against David; they had been best friends ever since they were boys. Even arranging your marriage to David was part of your father's obsession with getting rid of him, wasn't it?"

"I knew that, of course, but it didn't change the fact that I loved David. All I wanted was to be married to him and it drove everything else out of my head. He was that kind of person: you couldn't possibly imagine him not getting what he wanted or losing in anything he took on. In fact, come to think of it, I suspect that expectation was the very thing that drove Saul mad. The harder my father tried, the less he succeeded in removing this perceived threat to himself and to his throne."

"But what was it about David that made the king see him as a threat? After all, in those early days your father had immense resources and David had none."

"True. The only reason I can give for my father's reaction was that it began as an irrational fear of someone younger, more gifted, and—perhaps most threatening of all—much more popular. Royal courts are full of examples of irrational jealousy towards anyone who is a potential rival. It's not so different from the cutthroat bureaucracies and corporations we have today, where everyone advances at the expense of someone else.

"But you could also say that my father was not really irrational, because eventually it turned out that he was right about David. My husband was exactly what my father feared he was—a threat to his throne, to his kingship."

I sat back and looked at her. "I never thought of it that way. Your father was right in the end! It makes me suspect that the historian who set it all down at the time might have wanted to write your father off as ineffective and pathetic for reasons that had nothing to do with historical accuracy! He wanted to build up David by contrast and make him larger than life in order to prove that his kingship was inevitable."

"I wouldn't doubt it for a moment. Propaganda is much older than the century we're living in." Michal paused for a moment to collect her thoughts. "My father's plan was to exhaust David, to wear him down in the Philistine campaign so that, with any luck, he would be killed. At one stage he demanded that David come back with a hundred dead Philistines before he could marry me. David went away for a month with a regiment of my father's troops and arrived back with two hundred!" She smiled at the memory. "You should have seen my father's face. David and I were married within the week."

"Even then your father didn't stop, did he?"

"No. Sometimes we thought things had changed, and for long periods David was welcome at court. About the same time my father began to suffer from long periods of depression. There were lots of reasons: he knew he was getting older and no longer had what it took to be fully in charge. In those days, when any king began to get physically weak, everyone knew his reign was over—or soon would be. Music was the only thing that seemed to help my father; it cheered him up, calmed his nerves.

But he was still so unpredictable: one day as David was playing for him, Saul suddenly grabbed a spear from the bodyguard beside him. Twice he threw it at David, who dodged just in time."

"Were you there?" I asked.

"Yes," she said. "I will never forget the sound of the spear thudding into the wall where David had been a moment before."

"What did David do?"

"He got out of there and came home to the house. We lived nearby. I knew my father well enough to know that it wouldn't stop here, that eventually his strongmen would come for David. We threw a few things together, got him out of the house without being seen, and he headed for the hill country. I had to face my father alone. He was livid, and accused me of plotting against him. I thought he would kill me. The only thing that got me off the hook was my plea that if I hadn't cooperated, David would have killed *me*. My father believed it because this was just the way his own mind worked."

"David had other women during the time he was a fugitive, didn't he? In different places around the country?"

"Oh yes. He married two of them during those months on the run. But later, much later when my father and Jonathan were both dead, David returned to the city after the battle and began to consolidate his power. The first thing he demanded was that the army go find where I was and bring me back to him." She said this with immense satisfaction.

"After he took power and became king, after your father's death on Mount Gilboa, David married more than once. Did you stay with him through all that?"

"I did. You have to realize a lot of that was part of the myth of kingship, of being all-powerful. The king had to be sexually virile as well as a warrior. To some extent the royal bed was seen as an extension of the battlefield. There were a number of wives, not to mention concubines. It had nothing to do with bonds of affection, and certainly nothing to do with loving anyone. If love happened, it was a kind of extra."

"As with you two?"

"Yes, as with us," she said low and deep, dwelling on every word. It was moving to hear it. "I had to wait for him for long periods but he always came back to me. Even when I got furious with him, he came back to me."

"You were certainly outraged about his dancing half-naked in public!"

She smiled ruefully and shook her head. "Why is that the one thing that everyone remembers about me? So, I should have handled it differently, but life is like that. I saw his dance as sheer, crazy exhibitionism, and it wasn't until afterward that the truth dawned on me. On the day that they brought the ark of the covenant into the city, it was David the artist, the poet, the consummate romantic letting himself go fully and freely for one moment. It was David and God dancing together. I should have understood that but I didn't—and I was sorry ever afterward."

"Is that why you don't come into the story again? I notice that the storyteller says something cruel and dismissive about you just after he reports that head-on clash between you and David." I was being as tactful as I could.

"I can recall exactly what he wrote: 'And Michal the daughter of Saul had no child to the day of her death.' That statement has always rankled me terribly. It was meant to wound: in that culture the surest way to dismiss a woman was to sneer at her for being barren. Even the word is horrible. It makes you into a non-person, erases you from the story.

"If you look at the description of our fight, you see that David makes a kind of speech claiming that his dancing was before the Lord, not just before his servant maids. I realize now that this was true for David. But then he hurled the memory of my father in my face. I can still hear him shouting that the Lord chose him in place of my father as prince over Israel. It was at the end of this piece of reporting that the sly remark came about my being barren. That was the clincher. That was the end of my story."

I was not sure if she had finished. I stayed silent, waiting. Finally she spoke again, very quietly and deliberately, as if forming a thought not realized before. "I think I had failed him in not understanding that underneath all the posturing, all the ego, everything you had to put up with if you traveled in David's life, there was also a very devout, mystical side."

In her voice I heard sadness and regret. Then I heard myself asking, "In spite of everything, how would you like to be remembered?"

For a long time she said nothing, as if collecting her thoughts. "Now that I see it all of a piece, I realize that I allowed myself to be used. I knew this, yet I refused to admit it. I loved my father, but the truth is that he used me as a pawn in his struggle with David. The fact that I loved David was merely a chance for my father to use me as the bait to catch David. If you knew how much I loved my father, you would know how hard it is for me to admit that."

There was a long pause as she tried to take hold of her emotions. "I loved David. I risked my life on at least one occasion protecting him from my father. But you will never read anywhere in our history that David even once said that he loved me. Maybe in his own way he did, but he, too, used me as a pawn between himself and my father. The priests who wrote it all down also used me for their own political purposes: I am the 'other woman' to Bathsheba—who had to be rehabilitated for her role as Solomon's mother later on. Bathsheba is the woman who responds to David's maturity; I am just the impetuous relationship of his adolescence. She understands David and I do not; she loves him and I hurt him. She produces the next king while I produce nothing."

By this time she seemed close to tears, and the only thing to do was to let them flow. Eventually she recovered control, and began to speak more calmly. "I also think that no matter how much I was used by two strong men, I was also used in a very different way. I like to think I was used by God. I think that I was among the few people who forced David to see some things in himself that he had to recognize: that he needed others to depend on at times, and that he was capable of being extremely selfish and cruel. Maybe, above all, I introduced David to the truth that a person could love just for the sake of loving, without wanting anything else. I never wanted anything else, you know. I only wanted his love."

I kept quiet. There was nothing I would have dared to say. When she had found her voice again, she said, "Maybe I was used by God to help in the making of a great king. Does that sound strange to you?"

"Not in the least," I assured her, "not in the least. I think God *did* use you, richly and wonderfully."

We sat there for what must have been a few minutes, neither speaking a word. She stood, gathering up the folders and the day book she had brought to discuss her professional plans. Instead of putting out her hand to shake mine, she leaned over my desk and very deliberately closed the Bible that lay open. As Michal prepared to go, I remembered there were arrangements still to be made.

"We forgot to talk about securing a space for your reception," I reminded her.

She laughed. "I forgot completely! I still very much need it if you will let me have it."

"Of course you may have it," I assured her. "I'll ask someone to phone you about the details."

7

Joab

The Loyal Soldier

It was told Joab, "The king is weeping and mourning for Absalom." So the victory that day was turned into mourning for all the troops; for the troops heard that day, "The king is grieving for his son." The troops stole into the city that day as soldiers steal in who are ashamed when they flee in battle. The king covered his face, and the king cried with a loud voice, "O my son Absalom, O Absalom, my son, my son!"

Then Joab came into the house to the king, and said, "Today you have covered with shame the faces of all your officers who have saved your life today, and the lives of your sons and your daughters, and the lives of your wives and your concubines, for love of those who hate you and for hatred of those who love you. You have made it clear today that commanders and officers are nothing to you; for I perceive that if Absalom were alive and all of us were dead today, you would be pleased.

"So go out at once and speak kindly to your servants; for I swear by the LORD, if you do not go, not a man will stay with you this night; and this will be worse for you than any disaster that has come upon you from your youth until now." Then the king got up and took his seat in the gate.

(2 Samuel 19:1-8)

E very line in his rugged face told me this was not a man to whom you would offer a cup of tea! Not that I had much else. Crossing my fingers, I suggested a whiskey, hoping that the dregs in the bottle were still drinkable. His eyes brightened, and he nodded. "Sounds good. Good for the memory," he grinned, "or at least good for loosening the tongue!"

He picked up a magazine from the coffee table and I went out to the kitchen to find a couple of glasses. Looking for a casual way to initiate the conversation, I began right away while I was still fiddling around with glasses and bottles.

"What was David like to work for?" I called out to the living room. "You and he were together for most of your adult lives. You must have known each other like family."

I couldn't see him from where I was pouring our drinks, but I could hear him. "Actually, we *were* family, in the most literal sense of the word. My mother was David's oldest sister, so he was my uncle—even though there was such an age gap between brother and sister that I was slightly older than my uncle David. Remember that he was the runt of Jesse's litter, you could say."

I came back and handed him his glass and a bottle of soda. I had poured him a rather liberal drink in an effort to get him to talk to me. In my experience, senior military people tend to use as few words as possible.

"I had forgotten that tie. It makes me realize how complicated some of the situations were that the two of you landed in together."

"God, yes!" he said fervently, shaking his head and adding soda to his glass.

"Why don't we begin at the beginning," I suggested. "You first met David when he was a nobody, right?"

"Right, when he was being chased all over southern Judea by Saul's men. By this time Saul was getting really nervous about this young rebel and had decided to eliminate him while there was still time. So David and I teamed up. In those days we could sleep on the ground, climb rocks like goats, stay on the run for weeks, fight like…well, fight hard. David and I were good friends in those days, and we stayed friends for a long time."

"Yes," I nodded, "you two eventually parted ways, but it wasn't until you were both getting along in years. But I'm interested in everything in between. Tell me about the time after Saul was killed, when David became king."

"Hold your fire!" he said. "An incident came up before that, and it's important that you hear about it because it showed me something significant about David. I didn't fully realize it at the time, but I remembered it long afterward. We were running from Saul and his troops, down near En Gedi by the Dead Sea. We were hiding in a large cave, near the back of it. When night came, what do you know? Saul and a squad of his men came in to spend the night right under our noses! I was all for cutting their throats after they fell asleep, but David wouldn't hear of it. He knew it was wrong to harm a king of Israel. So he cut off a piece of Saul's cloak and we got out of there. Then—it's hard to believe—a few months later almost exactly the same thing happened, and David made sure that Saul knew afterward who had been right there while he slept. Saul was devastated, but by then he was losing his grip."

"So what did you learn about David? You said those incidents showed you something."

"I realized that David didn't have it in him to be a real soldier. He wasn't prepared to go for the jugular—there was no way he could have killed Saul then and there in the cave. As the years passed, I gradually realized why: David was too many things. He was a poet and a philosopher, a ladies' man and a lawgiver, and he filled many other roles besides. That inability to go for the throat— as he had refused to do that night in the cave—turned out to be important in later years."

"But he went for the throat, as you put it, when he arranged for Uriah to be killed," I prompted.

He looked puzzled for a moment and then he remembered. "Oh, you mean Bathsheba's husband. That was different. You see, at that moment David was desperate. He had made Uriah's wife pregnant while the man was off fighting David's war miles away. If that story had gotten out, think what would have happened to the army's morale, to say nothing of David's credibility."

"Were you suspicious when Uriah came back from leave and handed you the sealed letter from David—the letter that ordered you to position Uriah at the head of the army so that he would end up isolated in enemy territory?"

"Not at the time. I was shocked at the instructions, but I assumed that Uriah had betrayed David in some way. Ironically, I was even glad to see David prepared to act decisively. It wasn't until it became obvious that David and Bathsheba had something going that I recognized his true motivation. By then the campaign was over. People's memories are short, and anyway, that kind of behavior was expected in the upper levels of the court and the military. It was just a fact of life."

"You were David's commander-in-chief by then, weren't you? So obviously he still trusted you."

"Yes and no." I looked at him sharply. Joab's tone of voice was resigned, but slightly bitter.

"Yes and no? What do you mean?"

He leaned forward. "One thing you need to understand is that in those days the idea of family was more complicated than it is today. Yes, David and I were family. If you want to know what that really meant, look at some of the extended families holding power today in the Middle East. Being family did *not* mean that you didn't have your differences; you still had to watch your back carefully.

"I certainly found this out with David. For instance, after Saul and Jonathan died, we still had to deal with Saul's general, Abner, and a lot of loyal troops. We fought them and won, but near the end of the day Abner killed my own younger brother, Asahel. I didn't have any choice: I had to avenge my brother's death some day, even though at the time I couldn't, because we had to return to headquarters. As soon as I got back, I found that David had made a deal with Abner to reunite the country—a move that was politically wise but made me livid! I tried to persuade David that Abner would eventually double-cross him, but he was adamant so I backed off. I was just waiting. When Abner turned up at Hebron I came to meet him, pretending I wanted to brief him. As soon as we were alone, I sank a dagger into his gut and told him it was for my brother."

"What did David do then?"

"Produced a state funeral for his so-called illustrious ally. He could really pull out all the stops when he needed to, could turn on the flattery and the tears. And he made sure of something else—that I took the blame for Abner's death so that the royal hands would remain lily-white. He also insulted me behind my back, telling one of his cohorts that 'the sons of Zeruiah'—that is, me and my brothers—were too violent. David said this at a time when he was glad to have us to do his dirty work for him, work he wasn't prepared to do himself!

"You should have been there the day we took Jerusalem from the Jebusites. David was determined to make it his capital, and later on he would build a temple there. I never quite understood it, but this was the dream he had. Anyway, the siege of Jerusalem went on, and as a last resort the Jebusites faced us with a mob made up of every beggar and cripple in the city. You can't imagine how a couple of hundred people like that could look in those days of no medicine: old wounds, leprous limbs, cancers, an unbelievable cross-section of human misery. You see, it was the popular belief that if you attacked such a crowd, you were cursed. Well, let's just say that I decided to ignore the curse, and the others followed me. We'll leave it at that."

"I know from reading your history that the worst time of all was when David's favorite son, Absalom, conspired against his father and raised up an army to revolt against the king. You were caught up in that, weren't you?"

"I was, but once again it all goes back to what family meant. You could still get a knife in your back at the family dinner table! What hurt David most was that his favorite son tried to usurp his kingdom. And for no good reason. Absalom was next in line for the throne, but he just couldn't wait. Looking back, I think this was the beginning of the end for David. He was no longer young—none of us were—and it was one blow too many."

I knew we were getting to a painful area. "At first you tried to reconcile father and son, didn't you?"

When he spoke, his voice was beginning to sound tired and old. "Yes, I did, and for the reasons I just told you. I knew David was terribly vulnerable to political intrigue and, quite apart from the fact that the traitor was part of the family, I wanted to keep things on an even keel in the kingdom for political reasons. So I tried, and for a while it worked. Then one day we heard that Absalom had gathered an army to lead against his father, and I knew (just as I knew with Saul years before) that David could not do what had to be done.

"So we fought against Absalom's men without him, agreeing to send David news of the battle. The last thing he did was to beg me not to harm Absalom. I said we wouldn't, but I was incredulous—I couldn't believe David didn't realize that it would be political suicide to bring Absalom back into any position of influence."

Joab stopped, as if hesitating to go any further. His voice became softer and he stopped looking at me. I thought he had become a little drowsy but it wasn't that.

"You know the story. You know what happened. We caught up with Absalom after his mule had passed beneath the thick branches of an oak tree, and Absalom was left hanging. I think he must have been wounded, or he was just bone weary. I looked at him and thought of all that he had cost us in lives lost. Then I stabbed him in the heart three times."

He was looking into some far distance as he remembered. "I didn't actually finish him off; I left that to others. I suppose I wasn't able to bring myself to end his life. After all, I had known Absalom since he was a child, though I also knew that the now-grown child would finish us all off if we let him."

The last sentence seemed like a plea for absolution. After a moment Joab continued. "In a way it was a kind of ending for us all. David was devastated when we told him that Absalom was dead, and he asked for my resignation. I don't even think he knew that I had been involved in the killing."

"You resigned but you didn't resign. Isn't that right?" I asked.

"In a sense," he replied. "I had to save David from himself. He could be so naive and sentimental. Who did he replace me with? A fellow named Amasa, one of Absalom's generals, if you can believe it! Can you imagine anything more stupid? I pretended to go along, but I knew someone had to act before David got his throat cut some night or drank something fatal. I killed Amasa the same way I killed Abner years before."

Clearly this time there were no regrets. This was a man who did what had to be done. Some things were that simple and straightforward. I felt I should keep quiet.

Joab put down the glass, got up, and went over to the window. He remained there, looking out as he spoke.

"I left David, eventually. I still think I was right to do it, at least for the country's sake. David's other son, Adonijah, rebelled, and he asked me to back him. I assume Adonijah wanted my name on his list of supporters as a kind of endorsement. I thought a great deal about it and then said I would. It was the most difficult decision of my life—even though there wasn't much life left for me. In the end, David fooled us both even though he was dying. He left the whole kingdom to Solomon, Bathsheba's son. Suddenly all our heads were on the block."

"You died for that?"

He turned around and put down the glass. "By that time it didn't really matter," Joab said. "In a sense I had already died, because I had lived too long and seen too much. It was enough."

We both moved towards the door, and I ventured to put a hand on his shoulder as we stood there. "You were loyal," I said.

He held out his hand. "I was. At least I tried to be. Trouble is, being a soldier is not enough. Being a politician is a lot more complicated. I wish now that I had stayed with David to the end."

"As things turned out, it probably was for the best," I told him. "Thank you for this time together." Joab responded only with a slight shake of his head, as if he was still trying to understand life and its meaning was still elusive.

As I closed the door and went back to my desk, I suddenly found myself recalling an old Irish proverb I learned in school: "The floors of the king's palace are very slippery." Talking with Joab had brought this saying back. It applies to even the finest of people when they work in public affairs of any kind, whether in politics or business or any profession. Despite our best efforts, despite even the successes that come now and then, at the end of the day there is a sense of partial defeat that we must try to deal with, either by denial or by an attempt to forgive ourselves. Sometimes too much can be demanded of our loyalties, so much that it becomes difficult to make peace with the past, however well-intentioned we were at the time.

8

Queen of Sheba

The Royal Traveler

When the queen of Sheba heard of the fame of Solomon (fame due to the name of the LORD), she came to test him with hard questions. She came to Jerusalem with a very great retinue, with camels bearing spices, and very much gold, and precious stones; and when she came to Solomon she told him all that was on her mind. Solomon answered all her questions; there was nothing hidden from the king that he could not explain to her.

When the queen of Sheba had observed all the wisdom of Solomon, the house that he had built, the food of his table, the seating of his officials, and the attendance of his servants, their clothing, his valets, and his burnt offerings that he offered at the house of the LORD, there was no more spirit in her....

Meanwhile King Solomon gave to the queen of Sheba every desire that she expressed, as well as what he gave her out of Solomon's royal bounty. Then she returned to her own land with her servants.

(1 Kings 10:1-5, 13)

The last notes of Handel's "Entrance of the Queen of Sheba" died away. We had been sitting in silence listening to the glorious music. I switched off the CD and turned to my visitor.

"I'm glad I happened to have it on hand," I said. "Do you like it?"

"Why wouldn't I? It's all about me!" She laughed. With an ebony-ringed finger she pointed to herself. "But why? Why all this interest in a journey taken so long ago?"

"It may well have been long ago, but a lot of things have conspired to make it far more than just another journey. Probably it has to do with where you went and whom you visited. Not to mention the fact that both of you ended up in these pages." I lifted the Bible for a moment. "All of it has turned into high romance." It was my turn to smile. "You may find this hard to believe, but you are now a kind of myth!"

My visitor was amused but also intrigued. "High romance...," she murmured, as if turning the words over to savor the thought, "a mythic figure." Her eyes had left me. She was looking out at the distant bay and the mountains beyond the grounds of the residential college where we had met.

She had come into our community as a visiting faculty member of a seminary in Nairobi. For the first week or two she had participated in the summer school classes, and one afternoon she asked to see me. We began to talk of the church in her province, and from there we moved into the need for training priests and catechists in her part of the country. I had asked if there were any signs at all of an acceptance of ordained women. She shook her head. Then, as if coming to a decision, she said very deliberately, "I also want to speak to you of being a woman in that part of the world, but in a way that may surprise you."

A few minutes later I realized that I was encountering another of my visitors from scripture. We had been chatting for quite a while when I suddenly remembered that the Handel piece was among the collection of CDs I kept in my office, and I couldn't resist playing it for her.

"People have never ceased to wonder why you made the visit to Solomon in the first place," I prompted.

She came back from her reverie and looked at me again. "That's funny. I have never been all that sure myself!"

I looked at her quizzically. "Seriously?"

"Quite seriously," she said, looking a little put out. "Does one have to have a reason for everything one does? Haven't you ever done anything on a crazy whim?"

I tried to rally. "All right, maybe the question was badly put. Let's try again. As you look back at it all now, why do you *think* you went?"

"Well, let's go back to the day his ships first arrived on our coast. (He came to us first, you know.) My people were rather frightened of them, though we had some of our own ships, smaller and less seaworthy, good enough to stay near the coast but not really equipped for long voyages. I thought their fleet was wonderful. Some of my advisors were wary, but I insisted we welcome the visitors."

I knew it was the moment to offer tea. She accepted, and while I boiled the water and prepared the pot, she continued and I listened.

"Our lands included some of the coastline. We ourselves had gone both north and south along the coast, although we never dared the ocean to the east."

"The Indian Ocean," I called out, looking around the corner of the kitchenette. "Go on, I can hear you."

"Now and again we had other visitors. I presume they were Arab *dhows* from the Gulf, or even from India itself. We knew that there were lands to the east, but I realize now that we were not really a maritime people. We just didn't probe very far."

I returned with the tray. "Then the ships arrived. Milk? Sugar?"

She smiled up at me as I served her. "Both, please. Yes indeed, the ships arrived." Her voice savored the memory.

"Tell me, had you ever heard of Solomon before? I'm assuming from the record he himself was not with the fleet."

"He wasn't, but I had heard his name. Very little else. It was mentioned up and down the caravan trail that ended at what is now Aden. No details, just hints, usually exotic and always greatly exaggerated. Solomon had quite a bit of notoriety: if the stories were to be believed, he lived to the far north, owned endless palaces, had more horses and chariots than anyone could count, and ruled an empire on which the sun rose and set. You know the kind of tales people tell around fires or when a ship is waiting for a breeze. You men love to exaggerate your exploits!" She laughed lightly, then, as if sorry for this last comment, she continued quickly.

"I realize now that what really intrigued me were the stories about Solomon told by the captains of his ships. They themselves were not Israelites, but Phoenicians. We knew this because they had been south before in their own ships. Solomon hired them because they were the best in the business: he had the money and they had the maritime expertise. He had fitted them out at Eziongeber, far south of his capital at Jerusalem, down at the end of the Sinai. Then they had sailed south, hugging the coast. Even for the Phoenicians it was a voyage into the relatively unknown. I think they were a bit surprised to find us as organized and sophisticated as we were."

"Did they turn north again after visiting you?" I asked.

"Not a bit of it. We seemed to whet their appetite for more. You have only to check the cargoes they brought home." She indicated the Bible on my desk. "You have a list of it in your records. To get those apes and ivory and peacocks they would have had to sail well south of us, maybe even as far south as the Zambezi."

"So it was after their visit you decided to take the journey?"

"I told you it was a whim! I admit there was more to it than that, although it was I who first broached the possibility with my advisors. They talked about the possibility of expanding trade, which was always desirable. For me it meant a long dangerous journey, to say nothing of an extended absence with the risk of political instability. Then there was the image of Solomon, given to me by his captains. He seemed very different from the usual self-glorifying warlord so familiar in my world. Here was a man who obviously held considerable political power, yet who seemed at the same time to have terrific intelligence and who loved beautiful, costly things. How could I *not* be intrigued?"

"You weren't put off by the large harem?" I asked mischievously.

She took it lightly, as I had meant it. "Heavens, no! In royal circles that came with the territory." She looked at me above her delicately poised tea cup. "I wasn't a complete innocent myself, you know."

A careful refilling of cups and passing round of cookies allowed a moment of silence and a strategic change of direction.

"I haven't asked an obvious question," I said. "How did you get there?"

"With his crew," she replied. "They went off south, then on their way back they called in to pick me up along with a few others. We made sure I did not go to Jerusalem without some things that would impress whomever we would meet: some of our spices, some of our diamonds and other precious stones. The art of diplomacy required such gifts, and they were an impressive sight, believe me. We sailed up to Eilat, where Solomon had huge business interests to the north—copper mines."

"Yes," I interjected. "The Valley of Timnah. The excavations are still there. Beautiful place. Silent and lonely, but beautiful. You still had a long way to go in order get to Jerusalem."

"We had an escort from there. Already it was obvious that hospitality was going to be lavish."

"I know from this"—I tapped the Bible—"that you were quite impressed by the whole visit. According to the record in the first book of the Kings, after you had 'observed all the wisdom of Solomon, the house that he had built, the food of his table, the seating of his officials, and the attendance of his servants, their clothing, his valets, and his burnt offerings that he offered at the house of the LORD, there was no more spirit' in you."

"Of course," she said. "I was at a complete loss for words. Solomon's possessions took my breath away. And this may surprise you, but I felt the most impressive thing about him was not what he owned, but how well he had survived being his father's son, the son of David. A father like that could have destroyed Solomon with the burden of his expectations."

"I hadn't thought of that," I admitted.

"There were some obvious ways in which he bowled me over," she continued. "The new temple was breathtaking, and he showed me where they had already used some of our imported wood in it. And as a military installation, Megiddo was impressive. Some of our people learned a lot very quickly there. But for me, at the end of the day, it was the man himself. He obviously had the respect of his people. He was faithfully continuing his father's commitment to justice for the people. And he was deeply and genuinely religious—not just pretending for the sake of his public. Traveling with him, passing the time of day with him for long hours, just getting to know him as a person, made me realize that in his own way Solomon also had a mystical streak that he had inherited from his father David."

"But not the urge to power," I suggested. "The record seems to show this. He did not hold the kingdom together."

She thought for a moment. "I suppose I would have to agree. David would never have allowed the nation to break up into northern and southern kingdoms that way. Solomon had inherited power, but he wasn't really interested in expanding that power. The most he was prepared to do was to hang on to what he had been given. As we know, simply maintaining the balance of power seldom works for long, especially in that kingdom and in that world."

"You could include today's world as well," I suggested dryly.

I knew I had been given more time with her than I had any right to expect, and I was anxious not to trespass. But there was one thing I could not resist asking before we parted. "Do you know a poem by John Masefield called 'Cargoes'?" She shook her head. "Let me read you a stanza for you. It is very well known, and while it doesn't mention you, it has those ships and your kind of world in mind." I reached for my Norton anthology, found the poem, and read:

Quinquireme of Ninevah,
     sailing home from Ophir,
Rowing home to haven in sunny Palestine,
     With a cargo of ivory,
     And apes and peacocks,
Sandalwood, cedarwood, and sweet white wine.

"How romantic he makes it sound," she said briskly. "The reality was much grimmer. Can you imagine what it was like to be a slave chained to one of those oars in the heat of the sun on the Red Sea? It makes me shudder to think of it now, though we took it so much for granted at the time that we barely gave it a second thought."

"Speaking of changed attitudes," I said, "what do you see ahead for women in your part of the world?"

She shrugged. "Struggle." The single word was offered with some sadness, perhaps even resignation. I let it hang there for a moment before replying.

"Is that all? Don't you see any progress, any resolution?"

"Oh yes," she said, "there will be progress. There is already some, but it is a slow business. It's easy for you in the west to forget that there are deep links between things like social progress and economics. As long as you insist that we pay you back the huge debts we owe you, there will be very little social change. A great deal will continue to be carried on the backs of women."

"Obviously some of you are breaking through," I suggested.

"Some," she agreed, as she prepared to depart. "But, as it was with someone else we have been talking about, it's going to be a long voyage."

I stood up. "Meeting you, I have the strong impression that you will eventually make it."

She extended her hand and smiled. "Yes," she said quietly. "We will most certainly make it. We are used to long voyages."

9

Naaman

The Commander-in-Chief

Naaman, commander of the army of the king of Aram, was a great man and in high favor with his master, because by him the LORD had given victory to Aram. The man, though a mighty warrior, suffered from leprosy....

So Naaman came with his horses and chariots, and halted at the entrance of Elisha's house. Elisha sent a messenger to him, saying, "Go, wash in the Jordan seven times, and your flesh shall be restored and you shall be clean."

But Naaman became angry and went away, saying, "I thought that for me he would surely come out, and stand and call upon the name of the LORD his God, and would wave his hand over the spot, and cure the leprosy! Are not Abana and Pharpar, the rivers of Damascus, better than all the waters of Israel? Could I not wash in them, and be clean?" He turned and went away in a rage.

But his servants approached and said to him, "Father, if the prophet had commanded you to do something difficult, would you not have done it? How much more, when all he said to you was, 'Wash and be clean'?" So he went down and immersed himself seven times in the Jordan, according to the word of the man of God; his flesh was restored like the flesh of a young boy, and he was clean.

(2 Kings 5:1, 9-14)

His face was full and strong with deep lines from sunburn. He was somewhere in his mid-fifties, hair cropped short and slightly graying around the edges. He had not let himself go, although in the few hours of the flight he obviously enjoyed his food and liquor. There was something about him that put me on the alert, something in the voice that, although our exchanges were brief, had a note of gruff command. He was even reading a copy of Norman Schwartzkopf's *Desert Storm*.

In every flight there comes some moment when it is only common courtesy to exchange some small talk, even if both of you wish to continue reading or working. He closed his book, unfastened his seat belt, and excused himself as he squeezed past me. When he returned to his seat, he reached for the book again.

"You're obviously enjoying it," I ventured.

"It's great. I can't put it down. I know every single mile in that desert, been over it more times than I can count; so I can visualize his whole campaign. I even envy our friend here"—he tapped the general's photograph—"his ability to move troops around far more quickly than I could. In fact, I envy him for a lot of things we hadn't even dreamed of in my time."

By now I was sure. "Are you Naaman," I asked, "the commander-in-chief of the armies of Aram, whose slave girl sent him to Elisha to be cured?"

"I am." He extended a hand. "I'm still military but mostly retired, which means I get called in to consult from time to time. So you understand how frustrated I get! These young analysts—kids right out of school—their computers make it all seem like a video game, not the real thing."

"Well, computers or not, from what it says in the Bible, you were a first-class strategist. The story we have makes it very obvious that the king had total trust in you."

"And so he should have," Naaman said dryly. "No one else had produced the results I had. We had an army corps that was the best: unbeatable time after time. I had first-class senior officers, more money than I had ever dreamed of, a magnificent home, a beautiful wife....Then it started." His eyes dropped to his hands on the closed book, and in a much quieter voice he said, "My disease."

I waited for him to continue. "I didn't realize at first what it was. Did you know that leprosy is sporadic? So it took me a while just to figure out the patterns of its coming and going. And the infection migrates: after a while it would disappear from one part of my body and show up in another. I noticed that the stress of planning a campaign would only make matters worse, so a few days before a battle I would suffer agonies. When things were all over it would fade, but the disease never fully left me."

"In the end you listened to one of your slaves. You must have been desperate. She was very young, wasn't she?"

"Yes, Maha—we gave her a Syrian name—had become almost like a daughter to both of us. She originally came from our southwest, somewhere in northern Israel. The army brought her along with the other prisoners of war from some campaign or other. My wife saw her when she was put up for auction, bid on her, and brought her home. Esther saw something in the girl she really liked—maybe the fact that she seemed to have a confidence beyond her years. In fact Maha became a member of the family."

"So one day she tells your wife about a healer, someone who might be able to cure your leprosy."

"Yes," he said, "right out of the blue. They were in my wife's private quarters. Maha was arranging her hair, and suddenly she made this suggestion: I should seek help for my disease in her country. At first I was angry when Esther told me. I guess I hadn't realized the thing was even noticeable—I just assumed Maha must have heard the two of us talking. Then I realized that she had risked bringing it up out of affection for me."

"Just the fact that you acted on her advice says to me that things must have seemed really out of control by this time. Am I right?"

"Out of control is a good way to put it. Because if I really did have what I suspected I had, I stood to lose literally everything: to contract leprosy was to be excluded from your own home, your family, your position in society, everything. It meant a kind of social death."

"Tell me," I said, "after you saw the king and you both decided that you should go to Israel, I've never understood why you and the king decided to sit down and write that letter to the king of Israel. After all, Maha hadn't said anything about the king himself being the one who could cure you, had she?"

"That letter was a diplomatic necessity. It was bound to be reported that I had crossed their borders. If I, a military man, had not been able to produce a letter to the king, I would have been seen as infiltrating their lines. They were plenty suspicious even with the letter! But you're right. I admit that I tended to look to the king first to get things done for me. I naturally assumed that he was the only strong man in the area."

"And you found otherwise, didn't you?"

"You can say that again!" He laughed. "But back to the king for a moment. Read the passage in the Bible again sometime, and you'll see that the king of Israel was certain this was a setup on our part. As he saw it, my seeking him to heal my leprosy was a trap, a deliberately impossible request that he would inevitably fail to grant; then our chariots would roll over the border and take his kingdom. After all, the Israelites and the Arameans had been at war for years. I had a hell of a job persuading him that my request was genuine. Eventually he told me where we could find this priest or medic or whatever he was."

"Prophet is the word you want." I blushed at my own pedantry, but Naaman wasn't fazed in the least.

"I was never quite sure who or what he was. To my knowledge we didn't have the equivalent in Syria. He was a mixture of sorts: part advisor, part seer, part healer. I think the main thing about him was that he seemed to be in touch with"—he hesitated—"a god."

"You must have been appalled when you met him—or didn't meet him, as things turned out. He just sent a servant out to you?"

"At first I was flabbergasted—and mad! Here I am, a big shot in the military-industrial complex of my day, complete with troops at my disposal, Arabian stallions, the latest in chariots, a regiment of aide-de-camps, more money than he was ever likely to see in his life—and what does he do? He sends some underling out to tell me go jump in the nearest river!" As he told his story, Naaman continued to chuckle at the memory.

"So you just cleared out."

"I sure did. If I hadn't, I probably would have killed the messenger and gone looking for the guy who sent him."

"And once again your luck held, and again it was one of your servants who advised you."

He looked at me quizzically and paused a minute. "Interesting you should use that word. Servant."

"Why?"

As if he had not heard me, Naaman returned to his story. "Thank God I listened to his advice." He was no longer looking at me, and was obviously revisiting the long-ago day. "By the time we had turned around and gone back to the prophet's house, there was no one around. But somehow I knew—don't ask me how—that I didn't need anyone around for what I had to do.

"The men hung back as I went down to the river. They knew I wanted privacy. I stripped. My skin was blazing as it always did when I was tense or anxious or angry.

The strange thing was I had no sense of being a fool or a dupe. I had always been brought up to believe that every river has its god. In fact, in some mysterious sense, every river is a god.

"I remember I became conscious that I was in the presence of something stronger and more powerful than anything I had ever imagined. For the first time in years I felt a deep sense of peace. Far from being in charge, the one giving the orders, I felt utterly humbled. But the uncanny part was that I didn't mind. It sounds strange (if you knew me, you would know just how strange), but I actually wanted to obey whoever or whatever was calling me to the river.

"I stepped in and waded deeper. The water felt neither cold nor warm; it was as if a dream had begun, as if hours were going by, although in actual time it must have been just a minute or two. The sense of inner peace began to change into a sense of physical ease. The pain and the awful irritation had vanished. As I waded out I could see more and more of my own body, the way it had been before. I couldn't believe it—I had the skin of my youth! I shouted my joy. My aide-de-camp ran towards me. He had my clothes. The others were out of sight. I wanted him to see what I myself was seeing. I wanted someone to vouch for the fact that I wasn't dreaming.

"He looked at me astounded, then he did an extraordinary thing, something that he ordinarily would never have dreamed of doing. If he had done it twenty-four hours before, I might have fired him on the spot. He dropped my clothes, ran to me, and embraced me in a massive bear hug. Locked together, the two of us reeled to and fro, laughing our heads off. Gradually we calmed down. He ran to get my clothes and left me to dress."

There was silence. Naaman had not looked at me once as he spoke. He seemed to be returning from a great distance. In a calm, low voice he said, "Remember you mentioned that I had been lucky in my servants? Maha had put me in touch with the prophet-healer, and then my own servant had insisted I take his advice. Well, another servant came into the picture that day."

"Another servant?" I asked, puzzled.

He pointed to himself. "For the first time in my whole life I realized that I was someone else's servant, someone above or beyond anything I could ever be or even conceive. I came to realize why the prophet-healer hadn't come out to greet me. It was not the insult I thought it was: he stayed away because he wanted to point me beyond himself. He refused to encounter me because he wanted me to encounter his God, the God of whom we are *all* servants, even—God forgive me—those of us who are the most arrogant and the most blinded by illusions of personal grandeur."

Neither of us had been aware of the plane's descent, but suddenly there was the clatter of seats straightening and fold-down tables being clicked back into place. Our spell of intimacy was broken. After we landed, as we stood in the aisle waiting for the doors to open, I ventured a last question: "When you went back to the king of Aram, did you keep your job?"

"I did," he said. "Why do you ask?"

"There must have been the same strain, the same crushing sense of responsibility."

"For almost another ten years."

"Did your—did the problem ever come back?" I asked quietly.

"Slightly, now and again when things really threatened to get out of hand. But never enough to make life miserable."

The line began to move. We were being separated. He looked back for a moment. "My own theory about all of this is simple. I ceased believing that I was God almighty. And I found the One who truly is. Goodbye. Have a safe trip."

He turned, and we both went our way into the crowds.

~◌
10

Amos

The Visionary

Thus says the LORD:
For three transgressions of Israel, and for four,
I will not revoke the punishment;
     because they sell the righteous for silver,
and the needy for a pair of sandals....

I hate, I despise your festivals,
Even though you offer me your
     burnt offerings and grain offerings,
I will not accept them....
     and I take no delight in your
          solemn assemblies.
But let justice roll down like waters,
And righteousness like an everflowing stream.

                    (Amos 2:6, 5:21-22, 24)

The organization is made up entirely of cattle ranch-ers who range from Colorado to Alberta. Their objective is very simple: to give peasant communities in South and Central America the tools necessary to farm successfully. So every year they ship tractors south, some-times taking time off themselves to train the farmers who receive them. I had heard of the organization, but before today I had never met one of its members. I was asked to preach at a harvest service outside the city. At the potluck supper afterward, I found myself sitting beside a local rancher.

His ranch was nearby. What I immediately liked about him was his immense knowledge of the international scene; his articulate discussion of agriculture and busi-ness; and perhaps most of all, his obvious commitment to the world's need.

"People don't like to be told the truth," he said. "You would be amazed at the response we get in our organiza-tion when we make an appeal for our work down south. Some folks are determined to believe that it is none of our business what happens to other people!" He shook his head in disbelief.

Still feeling my way, I agreed. "I suspect it's because if we admitted certain things were true we would have to change, and that's the last thing we want to do."

He nodded. "The changes we need to make will involve sacrifice on the part of a lot of people, and that, my friend, is the last thing on their minds."

As the meal went on, I realized I was talking to a per-son of immense vision. At times he became passionate when speaking about his work. The evening ended with an invitation to visit his ranch.

So it came about that a couple of weeks later I found myself sitting astride what he had assured me was a quiet and utterly dependable horse. That afternoon, in the foothills of the Rockies, I realized that I had been given the privilege of encountering Amos, sheepherder of Tekoa, one of the great eighth-century prophets of Israel, and perhaps its most passionate advocate for social justice.

"Tell me, what made you do it?"

He was surprised. "What made me do it? God made me do it. It's obvious, isn't it? I said so time and time again. You'd have to be pretty dense to miss it."

"I know," I said, "but it isn't as obvious as you think these days. What exactly do you mean when you say that God made you do what you did, and say what you said? After all, here you were farming a comfortable piece of land, making a reasonable living, minding your own business, and suddenly you leave everything and walk into dangerous territory where you antagonize some very powerful people. Explain it to me. What were you thinking? How does God work this kind of thing?"

"All right," he said. "I'll try. But since I've never had to explain this before, it isn't going to be easy. Consider what was going on around me. My place was not that far from Jerusalem. That was the center of activity for the southern kingdom at the time; the king and the court were there. You do know that the country was split in two by then?"

I thought I detected a hint of sarcasm, but I merely nodded to let him know I was aware of the partition of Israel into north and south.

"That split had dire results. At first I was aware of this only in my own part, the south. Then there came a point when I could no longer stomach things. You can only stand by and watch your society rotting away for so long before reacting."

"Rotting? That's a pretty strong word! In what ways?"

"Every way you can think of. Most obvious was this: the rich began to get very rich indeed, while the dirt poor became even poorer."

"Hadn't it always been that way in Israel?"

"Well, to a certain extent you will always have social and economic differences, but the situation had become much worse in my lifetime. We'd always had laws in Israel that were meant to protect the poor—resident aliens, widows, orphans—but these were essentially moral rather than legal obligations. It's hard to give a short answer to your question, but I guess a large part of the reason for the growing disparity between rich and poor was the kingdom's partition into north and south under Reheboam, Solomon's son. Only one tribe, Judah, remained loyal to David's line.

"After all, show me a society that isn't impoverished in some ways by being divided. Americans fought a terrible war to prevent it happening. Canada is dreading the possibility today. And look at Ireland. Look at Eastern Europe.

"The situation was bad enough in the south, in my own part of the country. But for some reason I felt compelled to go north to Bethel. The call to do this was crystal clear. I knew it was dangerous, particularly because I was being called to the north for a purpose beyond myself and my own wishes. You asked me how God works this sort of thing. I'm telling you: when God calls on you to deliver a message, you go and do it in spite of your own wishes, your own fears."

"So you headed to Bethel, the great religious shrine of the north, and...?"

"And I found a society that was richer than it ever had been, and disintegrating. Not only were the poor falling even further behind, but the aristocracy seemed to want to rub their noses in it. 'They are selling out my poor,' the Lord said, 'for a pair of sandals.' Land grabbing—both legal and illegal—was widespread, and the justice system ran on bribes.

"But there was more to it than that. The social system was cracking open like an egg, but everything else was, too. Even the worship life of their temple showed signs of a kind of sickness. Although you could never prove it, I am certain the priests were part of the problem: they never asked questions about where the money came from or how it had been made. Worst of all, the more the rot spread throughout the kingdom and its institutions, the more elaborate and splendid these institutions became."

"You said so very publicly, didn't you?"

"Right in front of the temple. I remember hearing my voice echoing around the stone walls. But as soon as I opened my mouth, I knew these were not merely my words. Even though I said 'I' and 'me,' I did not mean only myself—and it was obvious my hearers knew this, too. 'I hate, I despise your festivals.... Even though you offer me your burnt offerings and grain offerings, I will not accept them.... Take away from me the noise of your songs.' I shouted that message out as loud as I could."

I couldn't resist breaking in. "Do you remember what you said next?"

"Of course," he said. "Do you know why?" I waited for him to continue. "Because this was the moment when I was absolutely sure of being God's voice in that place.

'Let justice roll down like waters, and righteousness like an everflowing stream.' The words were so unlike anything I could have said myself, the scope and breadth of them was so vast, they had to be God's."

There was silence between us for a few moments. With typical directness he broke it. "That day in the temple was my great moment, but of course nothing of the kind happened! No matter what I said, things went on exactly as they had been."

"But you must have been a powerful nuisance to the authorities—how come they didn't act against you, silence you in some way?"

"Because of the crowds. Like any society where things have begun to crumble, the powers-that-be know that their grip on things is fragile. Any time I spoke in the market places there were plenty of volatile crowds, and if anything had happened to me, there would have been hell to pay."

"Did you want to create an uprising? When I read some of the things you said I wonder. To tell the rich that they are selling out the poor for a silver teaspoon—that's pretty incendiary stuff. Did you want to set off a revolt?"

He shook his head. "That's the wrong question. I was not thinking in terms of what *I* wanted. If God had wanted a revolt, he would have brought it about. I said what I had to say and then I was done. You see, I realized after a few days just why the Lord had brought me north. He needed a voice—and I knew with absolute certainty that mine was to be that voice. The one thing that convinced me was that I had not sought out any of this. Instead, I was the one who had been sought out and sent here."

"Tell me about your meeting with Amaziah, the high priest of the temple."

"That was the high point for me!" He was obviously enjoying the memory. "I faced him down on the steps of the temple. I pointed to his city and spelled out in words of one syllable the injustices all around him. Then I pointed behind him to his temple and asked if its magnificent worship had anything to do with all the rot that lay around it."

"And he threw you out, didn't he?"

"Not before letting me know that he had no intention of changing a thing. Business would go on as usual. This encounter forced me to realize how much of my mission had left my own hands; it lay in God's hand. Someone other than myself had taken over and I was just the means to an end: I had no choice but to say what had to be said. When I spoke to Amaziah I had a feeling that someone else was talking. Someone other than me told him, 'The LORD took me from following the flock, and the LORD said to me, "Go, prophesy to my people Israel."'"

He suddenly grinned and added, "And I like to think that it was also the Lord who had me tell him that the wife of his king would one day be a prostitute for foreign invaders in the same places that she now did her shopping for linen sheets and ivory bangles!"

"What about the rest of the world, your oracles against the nations and kingdoms surrounding Israel? I've always been amazed at the extent of your mental map at that time."

"You mean the fact I didn't just concern myself with the locals?"

"Yes," I said. "Here you are, a small landowner outside a village like Tekoa sounding off about the Moabites and Ammonites and every other kingdom around you. How was that possible?"

"Look, Tekoa may not be your idea of a teeming metropolis, but it wasn't just a cow town, either. No place in the whole country was too far off the beaten track. Look at the map of it even today, especially the old caravan routes. One came up the coast from Egypt, heading for Damascus and beyond. The Way of the Kings was like one of your interstate highways. It ran from points south in Arabia, through Petra, and eventually went east to God knows where in Asia. Imagine what it was like to be brought up anywhere near those great lines of communication. Those caravans were like your airlines or television networks, the Internet of their day. All you had to do to brush up on current events was to hang around in the bazaars, ask questions and listen, and you heard what was happening—what people were thinking, all over the map."

"Think back," I said, "to those early days in Bethel. Remember when you had tried everything and there was really no response—at least none that you could see?" He nodded. "Was it that inner map that made it possible for you to speak to them about the future? Remember, 'I am raising up against you a nation, O house of Israel, says the LORD, the God of hosts.' Did your inner map help you to see what the rise of Assyria as an empire would mean?"

He shook his head. "No. You haven't really read or listened to the text you just quoted. You keep on thinking in terms of the personal, of *my* mind, *my* actions. I didn't see Assyria looming ahead—God did. Once again, try to hear me when I tell you that."

"You make me think of someone in this century who was somewhat like you," I said.

"You mean King, don't you? I know. I can imagine how he felt. I know his letter from the Birmingham jail; it was like listening to myself." He laughed. "Come to think of it, I've heard myself quoted in South America and South Africa, too, to name a few places!"

"Yes, but you remind me of Martin Luther King, Jr., for a different reason. It is not just that both of you called for justice in the face of great injustice, nor that both of you were ready to take great risks for your vision. What really links you both in my mind is the conviction you shared of being the servant of another who is greater than yourself: a servant of God."

It was time for us to turn our horses around and head for home and a meal. I thanked him cordially for his hospitality.

"Oh, I enjoyed it," he said. "But there is one more point. You didn't bring it up before and it's important—or at least I think so. As you know, I said a lot of rough things, harsh things. I think what goaded me most was the self-righteousness I kept running into. People in the establishment talked a lot about what they called 'the day of the Lord,' when God would come and put his stamp of approval on their lives and their society. They really believed that! Nothing I could say seemed to pierce that delusion. More than anything else, their self-righteousness persuaded me that there was no escaping a terrible future."

"You really lash out towards the end. Your final prophecies are chilling—all death and destruction."

"Not all." He shook his head. "Look at the last few verses. They are so different that some people think they're not mine! But they are." His gruff voice softened a little as he spoke:

> "The time is surely coming, says the LORD,
> when…the mountains shall drip sweet wine,
>   and all the hills shall flow with it.
> I will restore the fortunes of my people Israel,
>   and they shall rebuild the ruined cities
>   and inhabit them.
> they shall plant vineyards and drink their wine,
>   and they shall make gardens
>   and eat their fruit."

We rode in silence for a few moments. "Do you know why I said those things?" he asked. I shook my head. "Because the crueler the realities that you have to impart to people, the more you've got to give them some hope. Otherwise you bury them—they bury you!"

"That's wise of you."

"No, it isn't!" he laughed. "I'm not wise, not in the least wise. Remember me—Amos? I just prune the trees and shovel up the stuff that the sheep leave behind. Wisdom comes from up there." He pointed to the sky. "The amazing thing is that Wisdom can use somebody like me." His eyes held mine for a moment—strong, direct, confident. "Let's go and drink a little of that wine I was telling you about."

As we came out of the trees, we could see his house in silhouette against the mountains.

11

Isaiah

The Singer

Comfort, O comfort my people, says your God.
Speak tenderly to Jerusalem, and cry to her
    that she has served her term,
    that her penalty is paid,
that she has received from the LORD's hand
    double for all her sins.

A voice cries out:
"In the wilderness prepare
    the way of the LORD,
    make straight in the desert
    a highway for our God.
Every valley shall be lifted up,
    and every mountain and hill be made low;
    the uneven ground shall become level,
    and the rough places a plain.

Then the glory of the LORD shall be revealed,
    and all people shall see it together,
    for the mouth of the LORD has spoken."

(Isaiah 40:1-5)

Since Vancouver is a tourist city, you can expect anyone and everyone to turn up on a Sunday morning looking for a cathedral service. As usual, I had scanned the faces of the congregation during the opening hymn and it was then that I saw him: a little older and chubbier than he looked on the evening television news, but still easily recognizable.

When the service was over, and I had greeted him at the door, I noticed him hanging around as if he were waiting for the crowds of worshipers and tourists to depart. "I was wondering," he said, "if you were by any chance free for lunch." Although I could not figure out why someone so important would want to invite me, I jumped at the chance, and suggested a small bistro around the corner from the cathedral.

Of all my visitors from the world of the Bible, he turned out to be the most direct. Because I was not even thinking of the possibility of his being one of them, he took me completely by surprise when he said, "It must be disconcerting to find yourself face to face with someone you have always thought of as being in your remote past."

Suddenly things began to fall into place. I thought of the scope of his weekly programming: in television journalism, his beat was the world. As an interviewer, my companion had a great gift for getting the best out of his often distinguished guests; he gave every impression of knowing their situation through and through. I realized that he had a large staff briefing him, but he was also versed in international affairs to an extraordinary degree.

Then the moment of recognition came. He took great satisfaction in my pointing my fork at him and exclaiming, "Isaiah!"

He laughed. "How did you figure it out?"

"I'm not sure," I admitted. "But recently I've paid a lot of attention to you as an interesting voice in political commentary, even though I know you're not in politics. I've always been drawn to—this may sound pretentious!—the scope of your vision. You seem to possess a very large inner geopolitical map."

"Ah," he said, "and I bet that got you thinking about phrases like 'the nations are like a drop in a bucket'— something I once said long ago."

I was impressed. "That's exactly the phrase I thought of. I've always considered it a magnificent image."

He inclined his head slightly, accepting the compliment in the half-amused way I had come to like.

Changing direction, I said, "Let's talk about you and your work in my time—the place you have in national life. You've carved out a niche for yourself with your program. When you do these interviews with international figures and deliver your commentaries, what are you trying to achieve?"

"That's easy. I am absolutely certain that public opinion on this continent must steer away from isolationism. We grumble about how much the goings-on in the rest of the world appall us. But no matter how much we want just to concentrate on our own problems, we have to realize that we are linked to the rest of the world.

I could hardly wait to respond. "Is that similar, in a way, to what you were trying to communicate to the Israelites during those years they were exiled in Babylon?"

"Yes, to a certain extent. Of course, there is one major difference: this continent enjoys immense power and freedom, while Israel was completely dispossessed—had almost ceased to exist except as a memory in the hearts of her people. Still, I knew that if our people in Babylon became focused only on their *own* situation, their sense of identity would be destroyed and they would never get out of exile again."

"Is that why you are always talking about what you called 'the nations'?"

"Exactly," he said. Then, lowering his voice, he intoned, 'I am the LORD your God, the Holy One of Israel, your Savior. I give Egypt as your ransom, Ethiopia and Seba in exchange for you.' He smiled brightly. "Impressed?"

"Very, especially if I were part of a tiny people caught in a huge empire."

"Talking about being caught in Babylon, the reality is a bit more complex than the image many of you have of exile. You see, most of those exiles were quite happy. They had become so firmly established in Babylonian society and commerce that they hadn't the slightest intention of ever leaving, even if the opportunity arose. Remember that even though we were exiles in the Babylonian empire, we had Aramaic in common with them as the language of commerce. Aramaic was the English of that world, the *lingua franca*."

"What seemed to make all the difference was your insight that Cyrus of Persia would be the great liberator and savior of your people. Was that an inspired guess?"

He shook his head. "I wouldn't dismiss it as a guess, though I have always felt it was inspired. I don't say that to make myself important, but I honestly believe that there are moments and situations when God uses the human mind as a kind of door, an entry point into human affairs. Sometimes from the outside it may seem like an intuitive leap on someone's part, but the leap is actually God's leap. The human being is taken on a wild ride that leads to an insight. At this point we human beings tend to get the credit, but deep down we know that it happened almost in spite of ourselves."

"The idea of Cyrus was a huge leap," I replied. "Here you were, exiled in Babylon, down by what we call the Persian Gulf today—"

But he could not resist the urge to interrupt. "You realize how ironic it is that the gulf has that name today, considering that Cyrus himself was the ruler who brought the Persians onto the stage of history?"

"I do," I replied. "So here you all were in Babylon, in a sense prisoners in its empire. Then you, Isaiah, look out from this situation, mentally travel over a thousand miles north towards the Caspian Sea, and point to the rising Persian power headed by Cyrus. You suspect their potential, and then begin to tell your fellow exiles in Babylon that the Persians are going to set them free in the near future."

He nodded. "That's about it. Nothing energized our people more than telling them that Babylon itself was about to fall to the Persians! But believe me, it took some persuading. Many of them just couldn't get it; their narrow vision of God made it impossible for them to comprehend. They just could not see that something happening so far away from them had the remotest connection to their predicament as exiles in Babylon."

"Perhaps that's not so strange," I suggested. "After all, when you first began to prophesy of Cyrus as a national savior, he was half a world away."

"He was, and I was stretching people's credulity, I suppose. Besides, another reason the Persians came into the picture for me was that I had some helpful connections at fairly high levels."

"Connections? That's interesting."

"Oh, yes. We did have intelligence sources by then. Being exiled didn't mean that many of us had not succeeded in gaining influence with the Babylonians. The world did not have to wait until the twentieth century to realize that knowledge is power! I remind you again that apart from anything else, we shared Aramaic as a common language—and we also had some first-class minds they could use. As a result, I began to hear about anxieties that were on the rise in certain high places."

"What were they nervous about?"

"Security matters, mostly. Hints that all was not well on the edges of empire—or at the center, for that matter. I soon learned that the focus of the government's attention was on the Persians to the north; you call it Iran today. Ironic that now you in the west are nervous about exactly the same part of the world."

"So that's how you became aware of Cyrus. But wasn't it dangerous to speak as you did? Couldn't you be considered subversive in a very public way?"

"Subversive yes, but in public, no. I was very careful where and when I hinted at the possibility of a Persian takeover. As I said, my problem was one of credibility. It's extraordinary how small a vision of the world and of God some people have." We looked at each other, both knowing what the other was thinking. "I know," he said, "you have that problem today as well."

There was a pause while the waiter brought us coffee. Then I ventured, "What were you trying to do with the information you had, or should I say, your intuitions?"

"I was trying to give our people some hope. I was trying to prevent them from settling down so comfortably in Babylon that they wouldn't be able to respond even if given the chance to go home. As it was, many of them were already deeply part of the culture. I was trying to energize them for a future possibility that they just could not see. Meanwhile, because I knew that Cyrus and his troops were not going to appear overnight, I also had to give my people some comfort."

I couldn't resist doing what he had done. As distinctly as I could without being thrown out of the restaurant, I announced, "'Comfort, O comfort my people, says your God.'" To my surprise, he did not smile.

"There is something you don't grasp," he said. "Maybe it's unfair of me to expect you to. I don't think you can understand the pain of that exile. Today there is not the same sense of deep bonding between God and the nation as there was for those people. Think back to the shattering and the ripping away of the temple, the very place where God dwelled. Try to fathom what that might mean, to feel the utterly devastating effect of that loss on everything you were ever taught or understood about life and the world and God. Imagine your whole basis for reality being jerked out from under you. Then you may have some idea of the pain of those people and their need for comfort."

For a while there was silence. I felt foolish and a bit chastened, and he realized this. "Sorry," he said. "Sometimes I forget how hard it is for others to realize how terrible it was for us."

The truth was, I had been jolted into making a new connection. "I realize something about your songs that I never understood before. I think I understand why they would have spoken so piercingly to people."

"My songs?" He was puzzled.

"Perhaps I shouldn't call them songs—maybe 'psalms' is the best thing to call them. They possess the most heartfelt and lyrical language of almost any part of scripture. I know one of them almost by heart; it's from chapter fifty-three, and I suspect it's the best known.

> "Surely he has borne our infirmities
>   and carried our diseases;
> yet we accounted him stricken,
>   struck down by God, and afflicted.
> But he was wounded for our transgressions,
>   crushed for our iniquities;
>   upon him was the punishment
>   that made us whole,
>   and by his bruises we are healed."

He waited for me to finish and said, "I remember when I wrote that. It flowed from my hand as if it were being given to me from far beyond myself. I still believe it's true."

"All of this poetry is about a mysterious figure you speak of as a servant. The servant is always suffering. You return to this image again and again. We've never been

quite sure who or what you were referring to, whether the
one who is suffering is an individual or your people as a
whole."

"I'm very glad to hear that!"

His emphatic tone took me aback. "Glad! What do
you mean?"

"I mean that I am glad you've never been sure who
my suffering servant is. Do you want to know why?"

"Tell me." I was still confused by the turn the conversation had taken.

"Because I was never sure myself. Something was trying to express itself through me almost in spite of myself.
I suppose those songs—perhaps portraits would be a better word—still speak to you today because suffering
never ends, does it?" There was a wistfulness, even a sadness, in his voice.

"Take this century," he continued. "This twentieth
century of yours has probably seen more suffering than
any other. Certainly this was true for my people during
the thirties and forties in Europe. What I notice about a
lot of writing about the Holocaust or the Russian *gulag* is
how it becomes most powerful when it expresses the suf-
ferings of many by focusing on the suffering of one person, one witness. Think of Anne Frank's diary or *One Day
in the Life of Ivan Denisovich*. Both books tell about the
suffering of an individual, but we know that they also
speak to the suffering of millions of people who went
through the same experience.

"Like countless writers before and after me, I was trying to find a meaning for what had happened. I felt that
if I could give them a sense of meaning, the pain of
exile—or at least part of the pain—would go away. Or
perhaps it might become something creative and useful,

something that would build up rather than tear down. That's why my servant is transformed from being a victim to being a figure of hope."

I nodded. "I learned your words as a boy in school, learned them by heart. We used to recite them: 'He shall see his offspring and shall prolong his days.... I will allot him a portion with the great, and he shall divide the spoil with the strong.' I think they are in the same chapter you mentioned before."

He smiled. "What you must have thought of me in those days—one more piece of homework! The whole thrust of my thinking was to get Israel to see that their suffering was being used for purposes far beyond our human understanding. I truly believed that we were all instruments of God in ways beyond our comprehension, and that the price we were paying would become a gift to all humanity."

"I suppose you know that we Christians have given your hero your suffering servant a name and a specific identity."

"You mean Jesus of Nazareth? Yes I know that. It doesn't surprise me, considering he so obviously identified himself with so much else I wrote. In your gospels, I think it is Luke who describes in detail the day Jesus went to the synagogue in Nazareth. Jesus is just about to begin the few years of public life. He opens the scroll of my book and begins to read the very words I recall using to describe my own vocation in Babylon. There we are for a moment, the two of us, separated by centuries, yet both describing our vocation in the same way."

He began to quote the lines.

"The spirit of the LORD is upon me,
    because he has anointed me

to bring good news to the poor.
He has sent me to proclaim
    release to the captives
    and recovery of sight to the blind,
to let the oppressed go free,
to proclaim the year of the LORD's favor."

The words and the images were so eloquent I could well understand their galvanizing effect on the exiles in Babylon long ago. They have given strength and comfort to countless men and women down the centuries, people who have hurled themselves into the search for justice and liberation. I was so moved by hearing him speak these words again that I was not aware he had begun talking again.

"...so that way down deep, our longing is for liberation of some kind for ourselves, or our families, or society as a whole. All human beings are in some sense imprisoned, limited, held back. Whether our prison is physical or spiritual or political, it is always there. To be able to show someone the way out—to be able to lead a whole nation out of bondage—is to give a vision of liberation. I think this may be the ultimate gift anyone has to offer."

There was nothing I could add. I merely responded weakly, "Yes, it may be the ultimate gift. It certainly can exact the ultimate cost from the one who offers it."

He looked at me, saying nothing at first. Then he said, "Thank you. I think you understand what I was trying to say and do when I wrote those things."

"I think I do," I replied. "I very much hope I do. Perhaps my time and my society needs to hear your voice again. The strange thing about the longing for liberation

is that we long for it even though we seem to have everything we might ever need."

He waited, sensing my wish to think aloud. "Take us
in today's west. In many ways, we are free and liberated—
some would say far too much so—yet there is a widespread sense of being held captive or in prison. These
prisons are subtle, vast, indefinable forces and structures
that no one can get at. Even though most people—not
all, but most—have an abundance of material things,
there is this longing to be free from meaninglessness and
fear."

He nodded slowly. "At the end of the day, people long
for God, even if many of them can't bring themselves to
name the God they long for."

We were both silent, the kind of silence that signals a
conversation is coming to an end. We looked at each
other, both acknowledging the moment. I expressed my
thanks for the immense privilege he had given me. As we
stood and moved towards the door, I could not resist saying, "Do you realize that we Christians use your book
more than any other part of the Bible in our worship?"

Smiling, he shook my hand and said, "What a responsibility! All those things I said...."

"Believe me, they stand up well," I told him as we
parted at the door.

12

Nehemiah

The Builder

In the month of Nisan, in the twentieth year of King Artaxerxes, when wine was served him, I carried the wine and gave it to the king. Now, I had never been sad in his presence before. So the king said to me, "Why is your face sad, since you are not sick? This can only be sadness of the heart."

Then I was very much afraid. I said to the king, "May the king live forever! Why should my face not be sad, when [Jerusalem], the place of my ancestors' graves, lies waste, and its gates have been destroyed by fire?"

Then the king said to me, "What do you request?" So I prayed to the God of heaven. Then I said to the king, "If it pleases the king, and if your servant has found favor with you, I ask that you send me to Judah, to the city of my ancestors' graves, so that I may rebuild it."

(Nehemiah 2:1-5)

I had never before noticed the plaque high on the corner of the wall leading to the alleyway, although I must have passed it often enough on my wanderings about the Old City of Jerusalem. It informed me that if I went down the alley, I would see a small portion of the city walls as they had been rebuilt about twenty-five centuries ago in the time of Nehemiah. Having an hour to spare that day, I decided to press on.

It did not take me long to reach the open area. Some sporadic digging was going on there, probably governed by the vagaries of government or private foundation funding. I was so intrigued that I didn't become aware of the heavy-set figure standing beside me until he spoke. He followed my gaze down to where the old stones showed against the brown earth. They were smooth, very regular, and pressed firmly together.

"Not bad for a job that is twenty-five centuries old," he said to me.

"Not bad at all," I said, "but magnificent would be a better word."

"Thank you," he said, looking directly at me. "I appreciate that. I didn't get a great deal of appreciation at the time."

The message he was sending was very clear. I felt the thrill of making another unexpected encounter across time. I was still a little careful, however, not wishing to seem foolish. Extending a hand, I introduced myself, then asked, "And you are?"

"Nehemiah." He responded warmly to my hand-shake, and then his eyes flicked back down into the excavation. "As you may know, my speciality was shoring up old walls." He laughed. "Have you got time for a cup of coffee?"

Of course I did. We looked around the area for a cafe that wasn't crowded; he seemed to know the neighborhood better than I. We ended up in a small outdoor veranda looking northeast over the temple area, gave our order, and sat admiring the view.

"It's incredibly large now," he said without looking at me. "It bears almost no relationship to the place I came back to from Babylon. These people," he gestured around him, "wouldn't recognize my Jerusalem as a city at all."

"Yet you loved it enough to give it your best," I replied. "I know that from what I've read."

"Oh, yes," he said, "the journal I kept. Sometimes I was so busy it seemed a terrible nuisance. More than once I nearly gave it up. Now I'm glad I didn't. I was amazed to find that it is still around. It has even become some kind of sacred manuscript for you people, a chapter in the book you call your Bible."

"Let's start with the exile, in Babylon," I suggested. "You had obviously done well. You were a trusted figure in the palace, a cup-bearer with daily access to the king. Was it hard to give that up—I mean, for the job you took on?"

"I had no choice," said Nehemiah, "and that is God's truth. Many of us had kept in contact with people back in Jerusalem. Since I received letters regularly, I realized how bad the situation was and how low the morale of the survivors had dropped. The city was a ruin, the walls open to any hostile power, and there was no shortage of enemies only too eager to take advantage of our weakness.

"There came a point when I couldn't stand it any longer; I decided to risk asking permission to go back to Jerusalem for a while—or to what remained of it. As you know, I got a far better response from the king than I expected. Looking back now, I realize that he didn't want our city to become a smoking ruin any more that I did. It would create a dangerous power vacuum between himself and Egypt. So he sent me out with full military escort as governor of Judah, a small but key province in the satrapy of Trans-Euphrates. I was not to go back to Persia again for twelve years."

"Ever since I first read your journal, I've been intrigued by that solitary nighttime ride of inspection you took around the city walls. Why by yourself and why at night?"

"Because I knew I was going into a political hotbed divided into many factions. I wanted to see what damage had been done, what needed to be fixed, and in what order. When I went into Jerusalem and made myself known, I knew that the only way to operate would be by direct orders. Luckily the generosity of the king had given me the power to operate unilaterally. I didn't have to be democratic. Does that shock you?" He laughed. "More coffee?"

When our refills arrived, I mentioned something I have always thought of whenever Nehemiah's journal is read in public worship. "We have a wise man who lived in this century. His name was Reinhold Niebuhr, and I suppose you could say he was a prophet. He once made the observation that no virtuous act is quite as virtuous from the point of view of our friend or foe as it is from our own. For some reason I always think of that when your name comes up."

"I know what you mean," he said. "For a time things went well, all too well. But I knew trouble would come— if only because all sorts of factions and political parties had grown up both inside the city and around the countryside. I knew that sooner or later I would collide with some vested interests."

"At least you had the people on your side, the hard-working householder anxious to restore a decent way of life with a little security."

"Yes, I appealed to the ordinary people," Nehemiah said, "and they worked themselves to the bone for me. I wasn't easy to work for, nor did they realize how hard it would be, and how dangerous."

"Dangerous?"

"Very dangerous after a while." He shifted in the chair to get comfortable. "At first, those who didn't want the walls fixed applied what you would call psychological pressure, holding my workers and the other townspeople up to criticism and ridicule. They hoped to break the people's morale. Then, when that didn't succeed, they resorted to rumors and threats.

"There were three of these higher-ups trying to sabotage my building program. To the north of the city, Sanballat governed Samaria as his personal fiefdom, and it was very much in his interest to see that Jerusalem did not grow into a rival power again. He had two strong allies: Geshem, chieftain of the Nabateans, who ran things down south in Edom; and a rich tycoon Tobiah, who headed a huge Jewish clan with large holdings in Transjordan and allied himself with the powerful Jewish families that I was trying to deal with in Jerusalem. With Samaritans to the north and Ammonites to the east, we were completely encircled by enemies. I had to give every workman a weapon. We posted lookouts at intervals and had night patrols on duty."

He was looking down to the excavations as he said this. I knew he was back there once again, seeing faces, hearing voices, recalling certain moments. I let him break the silence. "The most dangerous threat was when they tried to accuse me of treason before the king in Babylon. It was clever of Sanballat. Capitalizing on the fact that the walls were indeed going up, he started a rumor that my real agenda was to complete them and then declare independence from Artaxerxes back in his capital at Susa. I knew that if the king had any suspicion that this was true, there would be hell to pay."

"How did you keep your balance?"

"Well, I suppose I bluffed it out. I thought I could rely on the relationship I had with the king. I just took the risk that he wouldn't hear, or if he did, he would trust that it wasn't true. But I can tell you I was worried. Sanballat invited me to a parlay in the same letter, and I very nearly went. Thank God I didn't; I probably would have been knifed in the back during the visit. As a matter of fact, a little while later I got a typically oily approach from Shemiah the high priest, suggesting I should take refuge in his temple in case someone was planning to slit my throat! I made it very clear that I knew he was in the pay of Tobiah and his family."

I noticed the flushed face and satisfied grin. Obviously Nehemiah was enjoying the memory of that encounter. "Well, you got it done in the end," I said, "and then you all had a big bash."

"Did we ever!" He threw back his head and guffawed. "That was quite a day. We marched around, we made speeches, we shamed the priests into blessing what we had done. They even marched in the procession. Even our worst and most powerful critics joined in: they knew they had to, or they would have risked losing the respect of the people whose sweat had gone into the whole enterprise. We ended the day in the temple, sacrificed God knows how many animals, and sent the sun down with a huge feast."

"End of story," I said, and was surprised at his reaction.

"No. It was by no means the end of the story." His voice was suddenly very serious. "We still had a lot of work to do. The hard part lay ahead. Building the walls turned out to be the easy part: building a society was ten times harder. We had to find ways of bringing in the people we needed from the surrounding communities. We had to set up a kind of militia to ensure continued security. And this was only part of it."

"I know that at this point you decided to go back to Susa for a while. Looking back now, considering how things deteriorated while you were away, do you think it was wise to go?"

"Wise or not, I had to go! I had no choice!" There was an indignant tone in his voice. I realized I had touched a sensitive area. His reply was loud enough that a few eyes from neighboring tables turned towards us. "It had been twelve years since I had been in the palace in Babylon. It would have aroused real suspicion if I hadn't appeared. As it was, everything turned out fine. Artaxerxes was getting on by then. He'd been in charge a long time. He was too secure to be easily worried or threatened by things on the far edge of the empire. I stayed for a few years and then headed west again for Jerusalem, where I received a real shock. You know from reading my book that things fell completely apart during my absence." His voice registered disgust.

"Was it about then that Ezra turned up?" I asked.

"Yes," he said, "and that made all the difference. Let's just leave it there, because we haven't time to get into all that. I'm not sure I would have had the stomach to deal with the mess I found waiting for me if he had not been there. I think we worked together well because we were so different: we were both builders, but of different things. I built city walls; Ezra could build up men and women into a people. What we had in common was the ability to be hard when it was needed."

The two of us stood up, getting ready to say goodbye. But at the end, I couldn't resist bringing up something that had always intrigued me. "The very last chapter of your journal," I prompted. "Remember it? The one where you list what you did to reform the temple and its priesthood?"

He smiled. "You're going to say it's out of character." I was amused that he almost seemed a little embarrassed. "You were referring to the quick prayer that I kept on saying as I wrote the last chapter?"

I certainly didn't want to embarrass him in any way. "You said it more than once, if my memory is right. 'Remember me, O my God, for good.' Sounds like someone hedging his bets, trying to make something all right with God."

There was a kind of sadness in his eyes I had not seen before. "I don't mind admitting it in the least. That's exactly what I was doing. You see," he glanced around and lowered his voice, "when you try to drag a whole people back to some level of stability and dignity, you sometimes have to make some very harsh decisions and do some very unpleasant things—things you never forget and you can't ever forgive yourself for…so you hope there is someone out there who can forgive you."

He looked away, and then, as if deciding that there was only one way to handle whatever painful memories had been awakened, he turned and walked off. I thought at first he would get control of himself and come back, if only to say goodbye. But he didn't. Nehemiah walked along the concrete causeway from which people admired the walls he had built centuries before. I noticed that he did not look at them as he passed by. I watched him in case he turned, but he disappeared into the warren of narrow streets.

My own feelings were confused as I sat down to think about our conversation. I am very conscious of living in a time when much about the Christian life—its authority gone, its unity fragile, its words largely unheeded—resembles a ruined city. To use an image that Nehemiah would understand, its walls are badly damaged.

Nehemiah's methods were so different from those that typify church life today, with its emphasis on striving for consensus, ensuring that all voices are heard, and a conciliatory approach to life and relationships. It is ironic that those parts of the contemporary church which seem to prosper are often unapologetically authoritarian, hierarchical, and uncompromising, and see the culture as nothing less than a battleground for moral and spiritual warfare. I did not have to wonder very long where Nehemiah and his colleague Ezra would stand along this spectrum.

My thoughts then went to the exile. I could not help thinking how the church today is basically in exile from the culture, banished to its margins. Nehemiah and Ezra had dragged Israel back to political and religious viability by sheer force of will. Some of their decisions involved pain for many people. Of necessity, they saw the surrounding world in an uncompromising light—a world made up of either friends or enemies with very little in between. The decisions they made were taken unilaterally and applied rigorously. In a word, exile was followed by a period of deeply conservative and authoritarian ways of thinking and acting.

I fiddled with my coffee cup, its dregs cold and pale. My encounter with this builder of city walls disturbed me greatly. It still does.

∾

13

Caspar

The Wise Man

In the time of King Herod, after Jesus was born in Bethlehem of Judea, wise men from the east came to Jerusalem, asking, "Where is the child who has been born king of the Jews? For we observed his star at its rising, and have come to pay him homage." When King Herod heard this, he was frightened, and all Jerusalem with him....

When they saw that the star had stopped, they were overwhelmed with joy. On entering the house they saw the child with Mary his mother; and they knelt down and paid him homage. Then, opening their treasure chests, they offered him gifts of gold, frankincense, and myrrh.

(Matthew 2:1-3,10-11)

We were into the second pot of coffee and he was actually beginning to smile, even to laugh a little. By now I could tell I was with someone who refused to take himself too seriously. "I'm not so sure I should tell you everything," he said teasingly. "By not revealing very much about ourselves, the three of us have managed to become much more fascinating and mysterious figures than we really were."

"Maybe so," I said. "By making that particular visit you guaranteed your place in history. When you set off for Bethlehem, did you have any idea what you were getting involved in? I know you thought that the child was somehow significant. Did you have any idea *how* significant?"

"We knew that something very important was about to happen, or at least our astrological observations told us so. When we set out in the first place, it was not to look for a child. For all we knew, we could have been searching for a general at the head of an army, or some royal reformer about to transform a particular society somewhere to the west of us. All we knew was that this would be important enough for us to keep an eye on it."

By now we were well into our conversation, talking more like friends than total strangers. But when we first met, I had no idea who he was. It was fortuitous that we turned up in the same place at the same time. A large conference on science and religion was underway in the convention center across from our cathedral, and I had been asked if I would open it with a short prayer. At the reception that followed, the stranger and I had started chatting. He seemed to wish to remain at some distance from the cacophony of voices that rose higher and higher as the reception progressed; I noticed the hearing aid in one ear.

We moved away to a corner that was slightly quieter and made conversation a little easier. My new friend was tall, bearded, impressive in the quiet way of people who are not trying to make an impression. He asked some questions about the church that showed him to be well informed; it turned out that he was the son of a priest. These days he was on the faculty of a major university, and in charge of its astronomical observatory.

As soon as we had gone off by ourselves, apart from the others, he seemed to make a decision. I realize now that he made his opening gambit when he looked at me a bit mischievously and said, "I often think that it is a very long way from a child in a manger to you clergy in your cathedrals!"

I wasn't sure how to take his remark, but realized that he was prepared to take my priesthood seriously. He had paid me a compliment by assuming that I could rise to the challenge. "But isn't it true," I said, "that the great religions of the world inevitably move from simplicity to complexity? This is true of more than religious institutions: the modern university and hospital are also a far cry from their simple beginnings."

He accepted this, was silent for a moment as he looked around the crowd, then turned to me and said in a very different tone of voice, "For me, the memory of that child has always been a haunting one. Not just the child, but the woman and the man with him."

A profound change came over him that caught my attention, as if all the chatting to this point had been merely a prelude. I tried to meet him halfway. "The child haunts us all," I ventured. "You can see that through centuries of Christian art. And you can see how we are haunted by the mother as well. As a madonna figure she is everywhere."

He waited until I had finished, nodded thoughtfully in agreement, and then said slowly and deliberately, "Imagine how haunted you would be if you had actually seen him."

I suddenly saw the chancellor of the university bearing down on us. It was obvious he was about to take my companion with him for some other purpose. While the chancellor was still some yards away I said, "We'll talk about this later," and moved away to free him for other people.

The following morning I went over to the convention center and found my new acquaintance was giving the opening lecture—his name was a household one in astronomy, certainly among his peers. I sat through his introduction and listened to those parts of his lecture I could understand. He talked a great deal about black holes and something called the Great Galactic Wall. At one stage, he objected passionately to recent drastic cuts in the space exploration program.

Later in the day, as we sat together in a quiet corner of the lobby of the convention center, I sensed some amusement among his fellow scientists that their colleague wished to give time to an insignificant priest who was there only to mutter some official prayers because the terms of the lectureship demanded it. As we talked, I was still curious as to his profession in an earlier time.

"So what exactly were you, if you don't want to be thought of as magicians?"

He thought for a moment. "Even then most people thought of us as magicians, but we had no such illusions.

When a gullible public is assembled and told that something is going to happen in the night sky, and it does, they naturally assume that those who told them about it actually caused it. The truth is that we were able to point out the star only because of the countless hours of calculations we had put into the effort. But," he grinned, "most of us like a little adulation now and then."

"So if you were not magicians—and I can see the word annoys you—what place did you fill in the Persian power structure?"

"Good choice of words: power structure. We were very much part of it. One prominent Roman voice—I think his name was Tertullian—later wanted to portray us as kings. But we were nothing of the sort. We gave advice and counsel to the ruler, but none of us wanted power. We were thinkers, intellectuals, and we all had different specialities. Some of us were astronomers—in fact we invented the science. Still others were philosophers.

"Some of us were fascinated by what astronomy meant for human life. As our insights accumulated, we found that we had a whole science on our hands. You people tend to sneer at astrology, but I can see that you haven't succeeded in doing away with it. I notice it in your newspapers and in those endless little books on your newsstands."

I merely nodded in agreement. He continued. "Using the word politics as you do, we were also accomplished politicians. We had the freedom and the public funds to travel, and we very often did. A couple of us, or a larger group, would head out from time to time to visit neighboring countries. We were not military, so we didn't come as a threat. We would use these visits to keep our ears open for any intelligence that might prove useful to our own state policies. Much of our work helped decide what you call today foreign policy."

His mention of travel gave me the opening I was waiting for. "So that's how you came to make the famous journey?" I ventured.

"That's how," he nodded. "Our calculations suggested a period of disturbance towards the west. That was our guiding star. We always kept an eye in that direction because of the belligerence of Rome. We knew, too, that even Rome could not keep the various Jewish factions from causing trouble, even under the capable hand of Herod. Furthermore, we knew Herod was very old and sick, so common sense told us there would be power plays going on all over the place to determine his successor. Hence, our celebrated journey." He laughed. "Of course, *we* didn't think of it as celebrated in the least. It was just another—shall we say—diplomatic probe."

"So you never expected to stumble on what you eventually found?"

"Not for a moment." His voice became more serious. "The reason we were in Bethlehem at all was to see Herod in the mountain fortress he had built about five miles east of the village. Even before we arrived, we got wind of the rumor: a child was to be born. It was all around the campfires at night. Every shepherd and herder we met had his version, and the women drawing water from the wells embellished it further. Someone even recalled a prophecy about a king being born in Bethlehem."

"I assume Herod had his eyes and ears around, too."

"Everywhere. His security people had heard it all. The only thing they did not know was exactly when the birth was expected. Every anticipated birth in the village was being watched. Anyone staying in the local inns as a traveler was reported."

"So far from being a drawback for the parents, Mary and Joseph, the cave under the hill was the factor that made all the difference. Is that what you're saying?"

He nodded. "That's exactly what I'm saying. If they had been given a room at the inn instead, they would have been registered and that would have been that." He looked at me squarely.

"Obviously you know what happened after you left?"

"Yes, indeed I do. Your world has its death squads and so did Herod. It seems they are always available when something new has to be crushed."

"Did you ever intend to let Herod know whether you found the child?"

He seemed to be searching for a way to say something. "What you've got to realize is that at the time, we looked upon all of this as merely local politics. We saw our role as observers. Our only reason for being there at all was to assess what bearing this coming change in Israel had on our foreign policy. Did it have any relevance for Persia? That was our only question. To be honest, I would have to say the child was neither here nor there in our thinking."

"But that changed? When?"

He answered very deliberately. "It changed when we met them, the child and his parents. We were getting ready to leave the area when some local herders insisted we visit this cave below the town. We could hardly understand them, but they were so adamant that we went." He was no longer looking at me. He was gazing into a far distance, seeing things I would never see.

"I will remember the moment until the day I die. There were three of them, two adults and a child. The father had cleaned the place as best he could; they obviously had nothing except the bare essentials. I remember an extraordinary thing happening as soon as the three of us got accustomed to the darkness. Without any conscious decision, at least that I am aware of, we found ourselves on our knees. All I knew was that I was in the presence of something utterly removed from anything I had ever before experienced—and believe me I had been in places of power, affluence, and wonder all over the world."

After a pause he continued. "I didn't know what to do or say. She sat there with the child in her arms. She must have been feeding him when we came. The baby was, well, a baby—a fine child, a healthy child, but still a baby. His eyes were looking up at his mother, his body was turning instinctively for her breast. The man seemed a little nervous, wondering who we were, whether we were a friend or a threat.

"It was at that moment that I knew we should not leave the place without offering a gift, and that whatever gift we gave, it could not be casual or cheap. I knew this with absolute certainty. I was about to turn to go outside to the camels when I felt a movement behind me, something being thrust into my hand. It was a small cache of gold coins we kept for general use. I realized that Balthazar, who was nearest the entrance, had slipped out to find our gifts in the saddlebags. Afterward my fellow travelers told me that they had felt with exactly the same certainty that we should give the parents something for the child. There was a small flask of myrrh and a container of some frankincense. We had brought them, along with some other valuables, in case we needed them for statutory gifts to various hosts along the way.

"I handed the gold coins to the man. He held them, as if not quite sure what to do with them. It was the woman who thanked us. I suggested to them they tell no one about the gifts; then we left. We never saw them again."

His gaze returned to meet mine. He was obviously affected by what he had experienced once again through memory. I felt that the only thing I could do was to leave gracefully. I thanked him and got to my feet. As he accompanied me towards the convention center entrance, he smiled as if amused at something.

"Yes?" I prompted.

"Nothing, really," he said, "just one of life's little ironies. Those gifts we gave: we had intended to give the myrrh and the frankincense to Herod as formal gifts from one court to another. When we met him, we were so disgusted and appalled that we substituted some lesser things we had brought—some manuscripts of poetry by one of our artists. So that's how the child got the other precious gifts in the end. The gold? We just happened to have it. We felt he should have that, too. To tell you the truth, we didn't know what to give him—somehow nothing seemed enough."

He held out his hand. We wished one another well, and parted.

14

Caiaphas

The High Priest

So the chief priests and the Pharisees called a meeting of the council, and said, "What are we to do? This man is performing many signs. If we let him go on like this, everyone will believe in him, and the Romans will come and destroy both our holy place and our nation."

But one of them, Caiaphas, who was high priest that year, said to them, "You know nothing at all! You do not understand that it is better for you to have one man die for the people than to have the whole nation destroyed....So from that day on they planned to put him to death."

(John 11:47-50, 53)

When [the high priest and the council] heard this,
they were enraged and wanted to kill [Peter and
the apostles]. But a Pharisee in the council named
Gamaliel, a teacher of the law, respected by all the
people, stood up and ordered the men to be put
outside for a short time. Then he said to
them,... "Keep away from these men and let them
alone; because if this plan or this undertaking is of
human origin, it will fail; but if it is of God, you will
not be able to overthrow them—in that case you
may even be found fighting against God!"

(Acts 5:33-35, 38-39)

By that time in the evening I was tired and exasperated—tired of my guest and exasperated at being con-
tinually put on the defensive. I had before me an
experienced politician with a brilliant legal mind honed
by decades in the public arena. To complicate things further, I could not shake off my childhood prejudices
towards this man whom I had first encountered in
Sunday school Bible lessons. There Caiaphas was always
the villain, the bad guy.

The reality was different. Of all the other faces and
voices that have come to me from the pages of the Bible,
none disturbed me as much as this man did—and for different reasons than I would have expected. It was not
that I felt myself in the presence of an evil human being.
Rather, I realized that I was in the presence of someone
of great ability, strength, and intelligence. My guest was
formidable in his faultless dark gray suit, not the least by
virtue of his utter composure and the steady gaze that
met me every time I looked at him. I felt utterly inade-

quate. I also knew that I was showing my insecurity through a kind of nervous anger, and I was helpless to do anything about it. Worst of all, I knew my guest was aware of it.

For some time we had been arguing about his role in the events that had led up to the crucifixion of a certain political prisoner. I use this expression because for Caiaphas it was a perfectly adequate way to identify the person who for many years has been, and always will be, my Lord.

"The fact is," I told him, "that somewhere between the proceedings in your house and those in Pilate's hall a few hours later, the charge was changed. You personally questioned the prisoner and managed to get a charge of blasphemy against him, but then you went to Pilate with a very different charge, one of sedition and treason. You told Pilate that the prisoner had forbidden the payment of taxes to the emperor. If the gospel record is true, this was a lie."

My visitor nodded. "You are questioning my decision?"

"Well," I backed off a little. "Even you can admit that changing the charge like that was devious. At worst it was dishonest. Why did you do it? Was the first charge fabricated to appeal to a Jewish tribunal? Because if so, it was hypocritical."

"My goodness," Caiaphas said, "you do throw words around. Now I am a hypocrite."

"You were the high priest," I protested. "That means you embodied everything that was holy in Judaism and in Jerusalem society. Your body was even considered sacred. In spite of this, you abused your position: you deliberately destroyed a man.

I could see that I had at last managed to pierce his detachment. Caiaphas shifted in the chair and leaned forward, looking directly at me. He spoke very deliberately.

"How can I get you to see that you have not the remotest idea of the danger and the complexity we all faced?" He managed to say it in a way that made me seem like some kind of innocent, stumbling around where I had no right to be.

"Danger and complexity? What kind?"

"Try to understand the realities with which I had to come to grips. One," he checked off on one finger, "I was responsible to the Romans for one of the most volatile societies around, one that was ready to explode for any reason, although usually it was politics, money, or religion. Two," again he ticked it off on a finger, "I had to work with a Roman official—Pontius Pilate, the governor of Judea—whose character was a most dangerous mixture of considerable power and great stupidity. His career before he came to Jerusalem as procurator had very mixed reviews; Pilate knew that the Jerusalem appointment was his last chance professionally."

"So did you!" I interrupted, regretting my words the moment I spoke, because they merely revealed my childish impatience and resentment.

Caiaphas did not react. "Yes, I did," he replied evenly. "It was my business to know such things, my responsibility." Again I felt he had gotten the better of me.

"I knew even more," Caiaphas continued. "I knew that your Jesus of Nazareth was becoming a significant figure in the complicated political mix that was Jerusalem. By this time, we had had a long succession of would-be saviors of the nation, all of whom had ended up dead on Roman crosses in very public places, most of them taking the lives of many other well-meaning people with them. I also knew of the much greater danger that Rome was becoming tired of the whole unstable mess. Furthermore, Pilate had been told that if he could not keep the peace during the Passover, the tenth legion stationed in Damascus would come south and do it for him. That would have entailed wholesale slaughter on a scale you can't even imagine."

"I do know something about that," I retorted. "We know what the Roman legions did a few decades later when they finally did come down. It was after your time, of course."

"Yes," he said soberly, "after my time. Let me tell you that I am not in the least ashamed of the means I used to prevent such bloodshed on my watch, as you would say."

"But didn't you see that Jesus was not one of your typical saviors? The record we have recalls him saying at one stage that his kingdom was not of this world. Didn't that mean anything to you?"

He paused as if choosing his next reply even more carefully. "Yes. It did mean something to me. It meant that he was the most dangerous kind of savior: self-made, beyond self-interest, and beyond politics. A fanatic, in other words."

Caiaphas' voice became even harder. "But you are missing the point. It did not matter in the least whether or not I understood the man called Jesus and whatever vision it was that possessed him. What mattered was how he was heard and how he was understood—or, much more likely, misunderstood—by the hundreds of thousands of uneducated wretches who were prepared to follow anyone who promised a better life and a better society. Remember, my friend, for most of those people a better life and better society meant getting rid of Rome. But only we who were running the country knew just how impossible that would be, even though we would have liked to do it ourselves!"

I couldn't resist. "I can understand why you wanted Rome to get out. Then you could have taken over yourself and brought your own people into power."

Caiaphas was unperturbed. "We certainly would have done that, but don't forget we had every right to do so. We represented the traditional government of the nation. There would have been nothing wrong in making that claim and carrying it out, *if*—and only if—we were in a position to do so."

"Let's go back to the way you changed the charge when you moved the prisoner to Pilate's court. In the trial in your own house you concentrated on the charge of blasphemy. The gospel of Luke tells me that when you brought the prisoner before Pilate you put the blasphemy charge almost as an afterthought. It followed the charge of 'perverting our nation, forbidding us to pay taxes to the emperor.' Why did you do that?"

"Simple. Because the blasphemy charge is the one that carried weight with our Jewish population, but it would have meant nothing to Pilate and he is the only one who could have imposed the death penalty. He would have understood it, but the point is that it would have been utterly irrelevant to him, and we would never have gotten a verdict from him."

"So you invented something you knew to be untrue!"

"It was far from untrue. You look back on all these events across twenty centuries of familiarity, twenty centuries of seeing this man Jesus through the eyes of your church. You people have studied every word he spoke. In the fields and the market places of Israel he could say all he wanted about the kingdom of heaven, but the heaven his followers were determined to find in his words and in his dreams was the heaven of political change and relief from high taxes. It was becoming obvious that to achieve those things, they were prepared to follow him to God knows where and into God knows what."

"Suppose Jesus simply refused to lead them that way?"

"Then he would not have been the first political dreamer to have disappointed his followers and been destroyed by that same disappointment and anger. What I am trying to tell you is that if we hadn't killed Jesus, they would have. You know as well as I do that one of his innermost circle—Judas Iscariot—began to have doubts even before we made an arrest."

I wanted to move on in the little time we had. "After it was all over...."

"What you really mean is, after it all began, don't you?" There was a kind of resignation in his voice.

"You must have been appalled when you realized it wasn't over, that in fact it was only beginning."

"Well," Caiaphas said, "there you go again, making assumptions because of what you know from your position in time. Always remember we were not looking backward as you are.

"What if a movement begins among you today, some radical movement with a plan to destroy and rebuild society as you know it? What will you do? You will monitor it very carefully. If it shows signs of getting out of hand, you will act—because you have to. If you don't, you will have all sorts of pressures on you. Supporters blaming you because you are not doing enough, opponents making political hay out of the fact that you are trying to be careful. Just the same with us. Nothing really changes in politics, believe me." He smiled wearily.

"When you first heard that Jesus' followers were making headlines in the days after his death—all the healing and preaching and general uproar in the temple area— your reaction was mild, to say the least."

"That was Gamaliel's doing. I was for lashing out strongly. I felt that we still had to nip the whole movement in the bud, and we could if we showed ourselves determined. But Gamaliel advised us to retaliate in a more measured way. You can read it in Acts: Gamaliel was convinced that if the new movement was not from God, it would fade away naturally without any help from us. But if it really was from God, then we were in trouble: we would place ourselves in jeopardy by resisting. And as you know, the movement did not fade away naturally— but considering what eventually happened, I suspect nothing would have worked to prevent it from gathering momentum."

"It's strange," I said, "that after you retaliated in a measured way to the provocation of the two key followers, Peter and John, you lashed out again with the death penalty in the case of Stephen. Where was Gamaliel then? Or did you decide he had given you bad advice?"

"I'm not sure." He seemed to have become hesitant in his replies, no longer as certain as he had been. "Gamaliel himself was a bit shaken when he saw the utter commitment of these people. They would listen to nothing, no matter how reasonable we tried to be. We had, of course, become the absolute enemy by having their leader crucified."

"I'm not sure I should ask this, but how did you react to the stories of Jesus' resurrection?"

"Oh, that," he said off-handedly. "Don't forget that in my world, stories of the resurrection of dead revolutionaries were run of the mill! The more desperate the cause, the more likely the rumor of rising from the dead. You know yourself that the very same things were being broadcast about John, the revolutionary they nicknamed the Baptizer."

"But to my knowledge, nobody claimed that John's tomb was empty."

For a moment Caiaphas said nothing. When he did speak, it was in a very detached way. "You and I could debate this subject until we are both sick of it. I could counter what you have just said by pointing out that merely because a body is missing does not prove that someone has risen from the dead. You could then respond by reminding me of the many witnesses who saw Jesus with them or among them. After that, we could debate the meaning of his presence for ever. Do you really want to do this?"

It was obvious that our conversation was over. And for good reason: we had come to the end of this man's participation in the great story. Again the suave senior official, he waved aside my thanks for the evening we had spent together, gave me an amused look, and said, "No, no, I am the one who should be grateful. After all, not many people get an opportunity to try to change someone's mind about the past. All I ask is that you at least try to report me accurately in what you write. After all, what else could I have done?"

I stayed alone in the room for a while after he left, a mixture of thoughts and feelings going through my mind. I still felt deeply disturbed by Caiaphas the high priest, but had to admit that I envied his self-possession, his utter certainty. The simple fact was that I wanted some of his strength and single-mindedness for myself.

In public life, the choice is rarely between an obvious good and an obvious evil, but usually between some mingling of the two. Looking back at an event with all the wisdom of hindsight is nothing like being embroiled in it, when instant decisions are called for and there is little or no time to think before acting. While I knew that I should condemn Caiaphas for his implacable enmity towards the person I worship as Lord, I could not help wondering if I would have acted any differently. The thought refused to leave me. After all, as Caiaphas said, what else could he have done?

15

Priscilla

The Community Organizer

Paul left Athens and went to Corinth. There he found a Jew named Aquila, a native of Pontus, who had recently come from Italy with his wife Priscilla, because Claudius had ordered all Jews to leave Rome. Paul went to see them, and, because he was of the same trade, he stayed with them, and they worked together—by trade they were tentmakers....

After staying there for a considerable time, Paul said farewell to the believers and sailed for Syria, accompanied by Priscilla and Aquila.

(Acts 18:1-3, 18)

Greet Prisca and Aquila, who work with me in
Christ Jesus, and who risked their necks for my
life.

(Romans 16:3)

The first we hear of Aquila and Priscilla is in this
account in the book of Acts, which portrays their ini-
tial meeting with Paul in Corinth. At first reading, the
passage seems quite simple and straightforward, yet a
deeper reading tells us a great deal. We learn the extent
to which this missionary couple was prepared to travel.
Given that Pontus is on the Black Sea, Rome is far to the
west, and Corinth lies between the two, each of these
journeys would have been dangerous, expensive, and
time-consuming.

Moreover, the reference to the emperor Claudius's
ejection of the Jews from Rome recalls the long experience of Jews with threats, intimidation, and forced
migrations. The fact that Aquila and Priscilla's business
was tent making, as was Paul's, made it necessary for
them to work not only in large urban areas but also in
places where there was the likelihood of a Roman army
garrison. The army had a constant need of tents. So it is
possible that Paul's visit to Aquila and Priscilla found
them at work on a large army contract that soon had Paul
giving a professional hand, and so earning his keep for a
while.

One of the nuances of the New Testament that has
always intrigued me is that whenever this couple is mentioned in Acts or in Paul's letters to the churches at
Corinth and Rome it is always the name of Priscilla that
comes first. In that culture, the order would normally be

reversed. Whether this tells us something about the pair—that Priscilla was the most energetic and forceful, for instance—we cannot tell. At least I thought we could not tell until the afternoon that I happened to be waiting for a flight at a large international airport thronged by a very cosmopolitan crowd.

I was wearing my clerical collar because it was Sunday and I had come straight from services in the cathedral. Seated near me in the departure lounge was a woman whom I thought to be in her early fifties. She seemed a seasoned traveler as she busily tapped away on her slim laptop. Two announcements of flight delays made it almost inevitable that we would make contact in some way, if only to indulge in a mutual grumble about airlines and schedules. And sometimes a clerical collar gives one a kind of permission to strike up a conversation with someone who is otherwise a stranger.

It turned out that she was rejoining her husband at one of the branches of their business organization, which manufactured computer parts. She went on to tell me about their involvement in the local congregation in Athens, and from there we moved on to talking about the church in which she grew up. She asked me about Christian life as I had experienced it. I began to detect a seriousness in her questions and observances that made me wonder if I had once again been given the gift of an encounter with one of my visitors across time. Providence did indeed seem to be at work: the seat beside her was vacant when we boarded, and she invited me to join her.

Looking back now, I am not sure at what moment she revealed herself as one half of the couple that looms so large in Paul's life and ministry. When she did so, I was (as always at these moments of discovery) absolutely overjoyed.

"What do you like to be called? Do you want to be Prisca or Priscilla?"

"It doesn't matter to me. Take your pick."

"Paul always calls you Prisca."

"Typical Paul! Always in a hurry, always breathless."

"The first thing I think about when I hear you and Aquila mentioned is how much I admire people who can carry their house on their back."

She looked puzzled, smiled apologetically, and shook her head. It was my turn to apologize: "Sorry. I mean that you obviously didn't mind constant travel, constant house moving—carrying your house on your back like a snail. It's an old phrase I remember from childhood."

Priscilla laughed. "I suppose we were rather like that snail of yours, now that I think of it. But remember in those days there really wasn't that much to move. At least, not as much as people manage to gather today. However, there were other reasons. Probably they're familiar to you from your own time."

I couldn't help noticing that her tone had suddenly changed from light banter to serious reflection. I looked at her, my eyes enquiring. I felt she wanted to continue. "Remember we were Jews," she said, the last word sounding slightly bitter. "Don't you think that's always significant?" The question was a kind of challenge.

"Yes. I know what you mean—at least I can guess. But isn't it true that the emperor had become fairly relaxed about Jews by this time? Some of you had even become his close advisors."

"That's true. But you know as well as I do that relationships like that are always based on self-interest. On the whole, they don't really signify full acceptance. Rome was always watchful and nervous about us, especially the more successful we happened to be."

"I suppose that the constant internal disagreements in the Jewish community didn't help."

"We certainly had our squabbles, and I have to admit that decisions like ours, my husband's and mine, didn't help." Her voice was resigned.

"You mean your decision to become Christians?" She nodded. The subject seemed to trigger memories. She remained silent, looking down. I couldn't tell whether her memories were pleasant or painful. It seemed best to focus on something else.

"Let's talk about Pontus. It is a lovely part of the world, especially if you are on the Black Sea coast. You two lived there for a while. I often wondered why. It seems such a long way off from—," I hesitated, looking for a phrase, "the center of things."

Her expression brightened. "Why Pontus? That's easy. Remember what we did for a living. We were tent-makers. You couldn't be in a better part of the world for our business. There were very few towns, but off to the northeast there was a lot of travel for commerce into Asia. Remember, that kind of travel took courage. It was lonely and dangerous, but there are always plenty of people who love that. They were our customers. We made a good product. They knew that our stuff wouldn't let them down, even in the very worst weather." She was smiling, proud of herself and her trade.

"But you left?" I prompted.

"We left for the oldest reason in the world: we wanted to better ourselves. And where better to go than Rome? We had been given a few introductions. We felt that with any luck we could make it, and we were doing very well until the emperor, Claudius, lashed out at people like us in the year 49. Overnight he decided that every Jew must get out of Rome. We all thought this policy must have something to do with the political tensions between Jerusalem and Rome at the time, but no one was very sure. All we knew was that we had to go. The irony for Aquila and me was that by this time we were no longer Jewish, in the sense of being acceptable to the Jewish community itself. We had chosen to become Christians."

"That made no difference?"

"Not really. As far as the Romans at the time were concerned, we were all Jews. You can't blame them, really. Jesus himself was a Jew. It was only logical to assume that this new movement was simply another Jewish sect. For those of us who chose the new faith, on the other hand, it was unlike anything we had known before. For us it had made all the difference in our lives."

I interrupted. "It excites me to hear you say that. What do you mean when you say it had made all the difference?"

She thought for while. "I'm not sure I can answer that. There is so much to say and it's hard to give a short answer. To me it's a little like being asked why getting married made such a difference. What do you say? Discovering the other person, making love, having a family, building a home? Each makes a difference, the whole thing makes a difference. Becoming a Christian was like that.

"There is something you might not realize—or then again maybe you might, considering some things happening out there," she said, waving a hand in the general direction of the world beyond the airplane window.

"One thing that made all the difference was that resurrection lived at the heart of what we believed. So many people at the time thought things in general were closing in, that all of life was coming to an end."

"You mean the empire itself?"

"Well, interestingly enough, the empire as a whole still seemed to be functioning well. There was no great threat from outside; that was to come much later. But there was a kind of tired feeling about it all: people becoming totally cynical about all the institutions of public life and their corrupt dealings; voices around dinner tables wondering where it was all heading.

"Then Aquila and I discovered a small Christian community that looked at things in a completely different way. To them, we were caught up in a new beginning, not a winding down. They believed that God had actually entered into history, so the whole drama had meaning. For the two of us, this meant coming alive in a new way."

"When Claudius's decree came down and you had to leave the city, didn't that dampen your spirits?"

"In a sense, yes, it did. We were beginning to reestablish ourselves and business was picking up. We had just landed an army contract for our tents. We were afraid we might lose it because of being Jews, but the local barracks commander said he didn't give a damn what we were: our tents were first class and he was sticking to the order. That cheered us up, believe me. But for the rest of it, we felt that God had some purpose for our having to leave Rome—and as it turned out, he did. We were not very long in Corinth before Paul came into our lives."

"And that changed everything?"

"Oh, everything! Suddenly we saw an absolutely clear road into the future. It was the real beginning of our lives. Paul stayed with us, as you probably know. Stayed for about a year and a half. Well, you must know how Paul worked. He turned night into day. People were always showing up at our place to talk more with him, to ask questions, get advice, find direction for their lives, anything!

"After a while we began to feel capable of helping him. If Paul wasn't there, they would talk to us. Sometimes he would bring people home with him and they would end up at our table, breaking bread with us. From there, it was a short step to staying around for an entire evening—and so began the house church."

She was talking faster, a little breathless, eyes shining, obviously living those days again.

"You had a house church in Corinth, and then you started one in Ephesus. Later on another in Rome. Clearly you were cut out for this. This was your ministry. How did all that sit with Aquila?"

She smiled. "You guessed correctly. It wasn't so easy for him. I was the extrovert: I thrived on a full house. Aquila wilted a little after a series of evenings. I had to pace things to keep him happy. In fact, I had to strike a balance between Paul's demands and Aquila's needs. Paul—well, you know Paul: completely single-minded. Family life, in fact, anything else, came a far second to the task of evangelizing."

"So, Corinth for a year and a half. With Paul as houseguest?"

She spread her arms, laughing. "Believe it or not! Can you imagine? Not only for that time in Corinth, but, later, for another two years in Ephesus! There were times we almost came to blows. But we survived. I think what made it possible was the feeling that we were all caught up in something bigger than we could ever know."

"And you certainly were." I found my own voice echoing the excitement in hers. "As you know, the communities you started are everywhere now. Oh, yes, there are problems. There always have been, always will be, but the thing goes on growing. What's so exciting for me is that we meet at a time when people are feeling the need for small groups just as you people did: for prayer, fellowship, and mutual support. In some parts of the world these groups are mushrooming for other reasons, sometimes for mutual protection in places where it can be dangerous to be Christian. So you were right about your house churches being a way to the future."

"I really wish Aquila could hear you say that," she said. "I would have liked him to hear someone bear me out about those groups. I could have said, 'I told you so!'"

I smiled. "Risky words in married life. By the way, tell me how long you were in Ephesus. You must have been there at least two years because we know that's how long Paul stayed."

"Long enough to get a good business going again. Paul came in with us. After all, even he couldn't talk twenty-four hours a day! Like us, he needed to earn some money, and he had this tentmaking skill on the side. Together the three of us were a formidable team!"

"So why did you pull up stakes and go back again to Rome? Did you just get restless?"

"Other people did—very restless. Things were never quite the same after the silversmiths' guild riot. Paul came within a hair's width of being killed. You can get an idea of how dangerous the time was by reading the account that Luke wrote in chapter nineteen of his second book, the Acts of the Apostles."

"Was Paul that much of a threat?"

"Paul? Of course he was! You can't imagine what kind of a driving force he could be. He was making deep inroads into a very lucrative business—the goddess Diana business. The stakes were high, with a lot to lose. Paul was lucky to come out alive. Our real fear was not so much about the uproar in the public theater, because the Romans always kept an eye on that kind of thing. Our fear was that he would end up in some alleyway with his throat cut."

"You played some part in all that, didn't you? Near the end of the letter Paul wrote to the community in Rome, he mentions that the two of you saved his neck in Ephesus. He uses that very phrase."

She made a gesture of dismissal. "We did what we could. We had some business connections ourselves that gave us a link to the city clerk and to the Roman administration. We told them the facts—that Paul had no intention of moving in on Demetrius and the silversmiths and their precious trinket empire."

"I thought that it was something like that," I said. "As you know, we have the record of what the city clerk said. He cut through all the bluster and the whipped up emotions, pointing out that this was a matter for the courts. That obviously cooled everyone's wish for a fight. It was over in a minute. Good old Roman administrative cool, you might say!"

The pilot's voice interrupted to tell us that we were beginning our descent into the airport. We had a few more minutes together, and I was curious why Priscilla and Aquila had gone back to Rome yet again after the years in Ephesus.

"I presume you did go back, because in his letter to the Roman community Paul greets both of you. As far as we know, he wrote that letter from Corinth before returning to Jerusalem for the last time. What I've often wondered is whether you two were in Rome when he arrived for his trial."

She shook her head. "You want to know whether he died in Rome or went on to Spain. We haven't time to go into it all, but let me just say this. You and I both know two things for certain: we know that Paul hoped to go to Spain, and also—something much more important—he went much farther, and still does. He always will. You can't kill people like Paul."

After we parted, I thought about Priscilla and the ministry she and her husband had practiced in those early days of the church. I recently read that between four and five out of every ten North Americans meet regularly in support groups of some kind, and that the vast majority of these are religious groups. They meet for prayer and Bible study, for mutual help in struggles with addictions, and for healing. If this research is even half true, it points to a significant movement in contemporary Christian life. Perhaps Priscilla and her husband Aquila should be regarded as the patron saints of all such gatherings. Some day I must compose a prayer that might be said when a house group meets, a prayer of gratitude for the lives of two magnificent people.

16

John

The Evangelist

Peter turned and saw the disciple whom Jesus loved following them; he was the one who had reclined next to Jesus at the supper and had said, "Lord, who is it that is going to betray you?"

When Peter saw him, he said to Jesus, "Lord, what about him?" Jesus said to him, "If it is my will that he remain until I come, what is that to you? Follow me!" So the rumor spread in the community that this disciple would not die. Yet Jesus did not say to him that he would not die, but, "If it is my will that he remain until I come, what is that to you?"

This is the disciple who is testifying to these things and has written them, and we know that his testimony is true. But there are also many other things that Jesus did; if every one of them were written down, I suppose that the world itself could not contain the books that would be written.

(John 21:20-24)

As I put the finishing touches to these pages, John the Evangelist visited for the third time in recent years. On two other occasions he had come quietly into my study, each time when I was writing either about our Lord or about some other personality in the gospel story. I speak of his visit as if he had arrived from somewhere else, yet it would be more fitting to say that I became aware of his being there, sitting in the easy chair close by my desk. One minute he was not there, at least to my knowledge, and the next minute he was. The pattern was always the same.

This time, after I had expressed my delight at his visit, I could not resist telling the evangelist what I was thinking. "Look," I said, "you must know that I am absolutely thrilled, not to say, honored, that you think me worth a visit. It's just that I am never sure what to call you."

For some reason I always find him very easy, comfortable to be with. He was smiling as if he found my surprise and pleasure faintly amusing. "What do *you* think I should be called?" he asked.

"I guess I'm more comfortable thinking of you as Saint John."

"Oh, why?" He wasn't in the least inquisitorial—that is not his style. Just gently curious in an amused way.

"I knew you were going to ask me why. I feel a bit embarrassed that I don't really have an answer."

"I know the feeling well. Believe me, I experienced it often with Jesus! Why don't you try? Sometimes the things we don't have an answer for can tell us something about ourselves."

So I decided to plunge in. "There's something about you, and about the things you write and the way you write them, that always haunts me. It is very different from the way I feel when I read Matthew, Mark, Luke, or even Paul. I don't know what it is."

"I think you and I are a little alike," he said very quietly.

I started to protest, but he insisted. "No, no, don't take it like that. There are all sorts of barriers between us that make it almost impossible for us to meet as two human beings, as two very fallible people. There's the time difference, twenty centuries of it. That's formidable. There's the fact that you met me in the pages of your sacred writings, which makes the element of sainthood you just mentioned even more complicated.

"All of that tends to cut us off from one another. So why not talk a bit about our similarities? I have a little theory that you should always take note of those figures in the Bible who really appeal to you. Try to get at the reasons why, to find out what you and the Bible character have in common. So once again let me say that I think you and I are a bit alike. Why don't we talk about that?"

I didn't want to seem like a coward, but asked, "Could you start?"

"All right," said my visitor, "let's see. You like poetry, don't you?" I nodded. "So do I. I found it quite hard to stay in prose when I was doing my book. In many places I was on the edge of poetry, especially when I was putting down what Jesus said to us. I think the reason for this approach is the extraordinary quality of everything he said: his words always seemed to ask for something else, something beyond themselves, layer upon layer.

"For instance, think of all the things I tried to remember from the hours we had together in the upper room. I don't know whether I succeeded in recalling exactly what he said, but I almost didn't need to. What was important was the meaning that lay behind what he tried to tell us that night. I may have forgotten specific words, but I could never forget the haunting quality of what he was saying, and the way he said it. You see, you don't have to apologize for groping for words! Look at how I am groping when I try to tell you about Jesus."

"I think I see what you mean about your being on the edge of poetry. When I was a child in school, I had to learn long passages of your book by heart. There was a time when I could begin with, 'I am the true vine and my Father is the husbandman,' and go on for most of the chapter. I realize now that the words have a kind of rhythm that made them easy to memorize."

"There," he said, "you see? The important thing is that you hear it and that it speaks to you so deeply. That's all I mean when I say we are alike."

He was immensely encouraging. I felt emboldened to respond. "I think I know another way in which we are alike. It's something to do with mystery. Your book is full of it. Whatever you write about, you always leave me with the feeling that there is much more to explore.

"Look at the way you begin. The other gospel writers choose some event that happened, like Matthew's wise men following the star, or Mark's description of John the Baptist. But you—you sail off into the end of the universe and then work your way back to where you started! The first chapter, for instance, which opens, 'In the beginning was the Word.' By the way, I learned to recite that by heart, too. I can still do it after all these years."

He was nodding in agreement. "I always remember just how hard it was to begin that book. I somehow had to find the words to convey that Jesus is a new beginning for the whole of humanity, that he is bigger than all of us, bigger than everything we had believed to that point, certainly bigger than the world he was born into. I remember despairing of ever finding a way to express that, until the idea came to me of his being what we called the *Logos,* or the Word. I was trying to say that somehow his life was an unimaginably potent instrument for the creative power of God.

"Here again is where words let us down. We both know what the word *Logos* means, but neither of us can conceive the immensity of it. Come to think of it, maybe that's as good a definition of mystery as any. Maybe a mystery is something that you have words for, but you have no idea of the vast content hidden in the words. It only appears as if the words contain the mystery. The truth is that the mystery contains the words, and it flows out far beyond them."

"I've known that!" I replied eagerly. "I've known it so well! You find some words and you are grateful for them as you scribble them down, but you know deep down that you haven't captured everything because—well, because who can capture a mystery?"

He held up a hand of warning, one finger raised. "I wish more people would realize that. There are so many who think the mystery of Jesus can be captured. They think it can be expressed and explained in words in the same way a machine can be taken apart and the pieces spread out to show how it works. They fault people like us because we are not precise enough: we don't define it all sufficiently. We don't write about Jesus in the kind of prose that reduces everything and tries to contain it."

I still felt quite shy about his suggestion that we two were alike. He must have seen it, for he got up and came round the desk where I was writing. "What is it this time?" he asked.

"To tell you the truth," I confessed, "it is something that grew out of our first meeting. Before then, I had never had a conversation across time, as we are having now. But after you came, it seemed as if I had somehow been given access to a wonderful doorway. I never know when these visitors are going to cross the threshold. For that matter, I never know how long they are going to stay."

"There's good reason for that, you know. It's not really in their hands." He did not elaborate, but kept his attention on the list of my visitors.

Afraid that I was babbling but unable to do much about it, I went on. "So, as I was saying, a number of people have come through and chatted with me. It's been the most wonderful privilege. Also a little frustrating, because I always want to know more, but there's only so much time."

"That's exactly how I felt when I approached the end of my book," he said. "I realized that I could keep writing for the rest of my life and I still wouldn't capture—here we go again—the mystery of the person I had tried to give my life to. So don't feel bad. We're all in the same boat."

JOHN THE EVANGELIST ✥ 157

He straightened up and moved back around the desk again. "I can't help noticing that quite a few women have come through your doorway," he said.

"Yes," I replied, "I never expected them to, but I found them fascinating. It's extraordinary how different-ly things appear from their point of view. I feel at a loss as I try to write up those encounters."

He nodded. "I still feel embarrassed at the way we treated the women who tried to break the news to us that he had risen, especially Mary of Magdala. We should have known she was as dependable as a rock. She had stayed through the whole horrible episode of crucifixion when most of the men had made themselves scarce."

"You only know that because you yourself also stayed the whole time."

"Well, the truth is that I stayed because his mother wanted to be with him. I felt I couldn't leave her. But the point I'm making is that it was inexcusable for the rest of them to dismiss Mary and the other women when they came with the news of what they had seen at the tomb. Luke did the best in his account, but Mark shortchanged them: all he wrote was that they were afraid and said nothing. Matthew doesn't mention the women at all. I knew instinctively that Mary was telling the truth, knew it every step of the way as Peter and I ran with her to the tomb. It intrigues me that you can go through countless paintings and drawings of the two of us running to the tomb without ever seeing Mary, in spite of the fact that I went out of my way to make it clear that she had come back with us. What's more, she waited around after we had raced off again, and so became the first to encounter the risen Jesus. All we could say was that the tomb was empty. She could say that she had spoken with him."

"I used to think of that when I had to listen to church-men argue about whether Jesus chose only men to be his apostles."

John stood up as if to go. "Thank God you people had the sense to work that out for yourselves. What were you thinking? How could you ignore the fact that he chose a woman to announce the very heart of the whole thing? If that doesn't make her an apostle, I don't know what would."

I changed the subject, aware that I never knew how much time remained or whether there would ever be another visit. "I always wondered why Peter seemed so threatened by you when you met together on the beach. Now I think I know."

He looked back from the door. "Peter was a strange person. A marvelous disciple, but an odd mixture of qualities: without fear but still fearful, ferocious at times but easily hurt, wise when he wasn't being, well, obtuse. He could never see the wonderful contribution he was making just by being himself, but then who of us can? He was dependable most of the time, faithful, resilient. Just having him there with us made all the difference."

For a moment he seemed ready to say more, but then he changed his mind. Lifting his hand in farewell, he said cheerfully, "Maybe that subject alone is a good rea-son for you and me to meet again sometime." And he was gone.

A moment later, though I could no longer see him, I heard his voice. "By the way," he said, "I almost forgot. Hope the book does well."